Benevolence and Blasphemy

BENEVOLENCE
and BLASPHEMY

*The Memoirs of a
Contemporary Art Collector*

J. Robert Orton, Jr.

TURTLE POINT PRESS
NEW YORK

© Turtle Point Press
Library of Congress Catalog Number 95-060520
Design and Composition: Wilsted & Taylor Publishing Services

Contents

Foreword

The art world has always drawn to it the most vibrant of personalities—the artists who create the work, the dealers who sell it, the collectors who consume it, and the museum curators who hang it are, more often than not, larger-than-life figures. Bob Orton, as a collector and a patron of contemporary artists, is one of those characters. In the 25 years that he has focused his attention on contemporary art he has had enough adventures to fill a dozen books! The reason is Bob has never been a collector who sits passively waiting for some dealer to tell him what to buy and then quietly hands over a check. Quite the contrary. Much of Bob's love of collecting has come from *the chase*—the interactions with artists, the wheeling and dealing with curators and gallery owners, the risk-taking of buying works of art that are underappreciated and undervalued. There is truly a story behind everything in Bob Orton's considerable collection. His stories are often humorous, more often ironic, and never dull; they exemplify the incredible reality of the very non-real world of art.

In the last two decades, Bob Orton has traversed the art world, making friends and enemies, but always leaving a lasting impression. Bob and I have known each other for much of that time, and there has not been a moment in those years that he hasn't made my life interesting. But, however you feel about him at a given moment, you are very aware that this is a man who feels passionately about art and artists, and about helping to push the limits of creativity and the acceptance of that creativity. The man's passions for art are real, the man's abilities are extraordinary, and the result has been exciting for all of us who care about contemporary art in America.

Dennis Barrie

Former Director
Cincinnati Contemporary Art Center

Director
Rock and Roll Museum
Cleveland, Ohio

Benevolence and Blasphemy

Introduction

For over two decades I have collected contemporary art.

It all began in 1970—my fiftieth year—when I struck it rich in my business and had disposable income to fritter away on impulse. Since age twenty-five I had accumulated exotic and sundry esoterica, always on a shoestring budget: Dutch "Cookie Cutter" art; Yugoslavian "Beehive" art; Etruscan pots; Japanese Ukiyoe prints; temple carvings from India, Thailand, Cambodia and Burma; West African tribal art; Chinese snuff bottles and Han Dynasty figurines, as well as Mexican pre-Columbian ceramic objects.

Atypically I gave hundreds of art pieces to museums, family, friends, customers and suppliers as I acquired them; today I have only a few prime examples I particularly like for their aesthetic appeal—or because they evoke pleasant memories of past travels. Almost without exception, I bought everything in the country of origin as I roamed the world on business. I observed one inflexible rule: Never store anything in a closet; if our house had no extra room, something had to go.

Once I got a bit exuberant and shipped home an excessive number of Indo-Chinese carvings, which pretty well exhausted our floor space. My intolerant wife protested vociferously. William Wolff—the eminent New York antiquarian and a friend—rescued me by conducting a successful sale of my precious objects at his prestigious Madison Avenue shop.

I have come to realize that I do not have the qualifications to be a real COLLECTOR. While I enjoy the challenge of selecting an object and buying it, the moment I have it I start thinking of how to get rid of it. I lack a desire to own things and feel a keen sense of relief when an object and I part company forever. In my heyday of buying contemporary art—my collection became known as the RSM Collection, named after the family business—the logistics of keeping track of hundreds of paintings, sculptures and photographs nearly sank us. We kept track of everything on an office computer, which wasn't too difficult, but we usually had twenty or more works on loan to galleries and museums at any time, which entailed packing, unpacking, shipping and insuring. Luckily I owned the corporation, so the staff had to do my bidding; but when I finally "cleaned house" and gave almost everything away to the Cincinnati Art Museum and other institutions, I breathed a great sigh of contentment to be rid of an unwanted burden.

On several occasions I have served as panelist in a public discussion on "How to Collect Contemporary Art," usually joined by museum personnel and dealers. My purpose in doing so is to encourage individuals and (small) corporations to involve themselves in the visual arts. My thesis is that one can spend a modest sum annually and over a period of time end up with a reasonably impressive aggregate, but it takes constant exposure to the current scene, with a corresponding commitment to educating one's self about "emerging" artists. I had to study the body of work of each individual in order to select the best and most typical examples.

Invariably, I was asked by those in the audience what kind of monetary return one could expect from investing in art. When I responded that I never bought art for that reason, the attendees shook their heads in disbelief. I hastened to explain that for a number of years I had a budget of $7,000 per year—later increased to $20,000—and at no time did I ever pay more than $7,000 for a single item. My estimate would be that in twenty years the collection would be appraised at twenty times the initial cost, providing I made astute choices. I concede only that art is a fine hedge against inflation.

1

How It All Began

Several people sparked my interest in art: A maternal first cousin, Jim Rorimer, nurtured my taste for the medieval period, when he reassembled from Europe the Cloisters—with Rockefeller money—at the northern tip of Manhattan. It was a branch of the Metropolitan Art Museum and this achievement led to his being appointed director there after World War II. In the mid-1930s, while attending Lawrenceville School in New Jersey, I would spend weekends with Jim (and his sister Louise), receiving an inspiring indoctrination into the world of art.

At the end of WW II, I spent several years in Florence, Italy, and fell under the spell of Bernard Berenson. As a young man he had created the Isabella Stewart Gardner Collection in Boston, and his residence, I Tatti, in Settignano, was a treasure trove of great paintings and sculpture (now a museum and study center owned by Harvard University). Berenson took a liking to me and shared prodigiously his knowledge and taste; I would visit often, perusing his outstanding library, gazing at his masterpieces and enjoying stimulating conversation at his excellent board. He would guide me around Florentine churches and museums, heightening my awareness with his reactions to what we viewed. After that I resolved to make a museum career of Central Italian art but, for a variety of reasons—partly economic, partly from war fatigue—it never came to pass.

A third influence was my friend George Rosenthal, who started buying contemporary art in the early 1950s. His principal advisor was Sidney Janis in New York, who showed many up-and-coming young people in his gallery. George had a great eye, but always seemed unsure about spending money on what today seem incredible bargains. His wife, Jean, and I would urge him to splurge on amounts he could easily afford.

I recall his paying $400 apiece for a fine Ferdinand Leger and a Jackson Pollack painting. For very little money the Rosenthals built a splendid collection, whose formation I enjoyed vicariously.

Meanwhile, to humor my Roman wife, Nori, whom I had wed shortly after WW II, I invested far larger amounts in paintings by Francesco Guardi, Pietro Longhi and Lucas Cranach the Elder—all most conservative, respectable choices (also very inexpensive in the immediate postwar era). For many years I paid monthly installments on those obligations.

A few times I deviated and once spent the princely sum of $150 for a pair of shadow boxes by Kurt Schwitters, whom I admired greatly. I had no surplus income and had to supplement my pathetic salary from RSM by winnings at the card table just to make ends meet.

These early art collecting experiences whetted my appetite, which had to be realistically economized by my accumulating trivial, unusual objects—which I did, over almost twenty years. By the time RSM provided copious amounts of money for me by 1970, I had no desire to buy anything for myself, but it did appeal to contribute something to my city that might have a lasting effect. I targeted the Cincinnati Art Museum for my munificence, because it was a dowdy, uninspiring institution that sorely needed shaking up. Since there was no permanent repository for contemporary art in Cincinnati, I set out to assemble a body of work reflecting the current scene, which the unimaginative director could not easily refuse.

Since 1939 Cincinnati has had a Contemporary Art Center which, although lively today, has a limited permanent collection, compiled more or less by accident. If only someone had been farsighted enough years ago to purchase even *one* outstanding work from each CAC show, the city today would undoubtedly have the most outstanding contemporary collection in the country.

Not having the foggiest notion as to how to initiate my project, I asked Robert Stearns, the director of the CAC, for guidance. He and my cousin Anne Rorimer (Jim's daughter), then curator of contemporary art at the Chicago Art Institute, both came to my rescue, offering inestimable advice. Rather uncharitably, each of them expressed qualms about my being able to make a transition from Renaissance to today's sensibility, somewhat corroborated when Bob urged that I start off by buying a Dan Flavin fluorescent light "Sculpture" as an opener. The thought that I would spend $5,000 for a scramble of neon tubes had even open-minded *me* in a state of shock! I foolishly declined the suggestion.

Today I still have Anne's kind letter, suggesting key New York dealers whom I should know. I didn't realize at the time that many had opened in Soho not long before. Principal on her list were John Weber (Gallery), Paula Cooper (Gallery), as well as Castelli and Sonnabend Galleries. Uptown were Blum Helman and Marian Goodman Galleries, who had recently opened a small viewing space on 57th Street, supplementing Multiples, a flourishing print publishing business. With Anne's entree, many of these dealers gave prodigiously of their time and knowledge to further my education, even though I bought nothing for two years. The contemporary field was so overwhelming I didn't know how or where to begin.

Anne Rorimer had curated a landmark show, "Europe in the '70s," which introduced important artists from the continent who were almost entirely unknown in the U.S. When it toured Cincinnati, Anne came for the opening and I had a chance to meet a number of those in the exhibit. Later I bought quite a few works by Ger Van Elk, Marcel Broodthaers, Richard Long, as well as by Hilla and Bernd Becher.

In time, I began to sort things out a bit and set priorities as to which artists' work I should buy. Over two years I visited museums and galleries in New York at least eight times and in Europe at least twice annually. In Copenhagen I became a friend of Steingrim Laursen, now director of the great Louisiana Museum. He, as much as anyone, provided a useful overview of the dynamic art being produced in Europe and the States, helping to sharpen my wits and refine my taste. In New York I became acquainted with Cora Rosevear, curator at MOMA, who provided continuing support to my endeavor; no one was more conversant with the contemporary scene. Even when we became close friends, she would never give me specific advice, but continuously pointed me in the right direction.

I found myself in a wonderful new world and read reams of material pertaining to the artists then emerging—in hindsight the *least* productive way I could have chosen to spend my time. Much better was to view the art and talk with those anxious to share enthusiasm and perspective.

10

When I finally summoned the courage to actually buy, I acted boldly and gained momentum with time, never worrying about making a mistake. In the course of making hundreds of decisions, I necessarily had lapses in judgment, and over time my taste would change or a work of art would "wear badly." I would trade off what I no longer wanted, replacing the object with what I preferred.

In the early 1970s my annual budget of $7,000 per year was overly limiting for my purposes, although in my first year of operation I trebled the amount, since I had bought nothing for two years of my program. The bulk of my purchases began in the later '70s, when I tripled my annual expenditure (exceeding that modestly on occasion) and continued on until 1986, when I gave the bulk of the collection to the Cincinnati Art Museum.

While I don't wish to denigrate the efforts of many dealers who helped me at that time, there just weren't many buyers of contemporary art when I began. It behooved them to cultivate a prospective collector who might develop into an important client. A dozen years later, when the art market was "hot," I could comb the New York galleries and only a handful of so-called friends would greet me or bother to converse. By then they knew I was a pipsqueak collector who would never pay inflated prices and was unworthy of attention. With pleasure, I note in particular that Paula Cooper and Marian Goodman were loyal exceptions.

From 1955 to 1970, prices had risen substantially. Still, a lot of wonderful art could be bought for reasonable sums of money. Most of the young dealers had art degrees from prominent universities and had worked either in museums or for older dealers, who had trained them well. Starting out for themselves was an act of great courage. Only someone truly passionate about art would possibly open a gallery. With existing prices, one had to sell a lot of art to pay the overhead and draw a living wage. The hours were grueling and often frustrating as one catered to collectors and continually humored temperamental artists. In some cases a freshman dealer had a collector as silent partner, who provided a necessary infusion of start-up capital in the hope of purchasing art at "wholesale" prices; rarely did this collaboration work successfully, as the art dealer had another constituency to cater to, who constantly and critically breathed down his/her neck.

Later on, I became a consultant to various New York

dealers, trying to help them run their operations in a businesslike manner. It gave me a unique insight into the workings of the art world, and led to the conclusion that under no circumstance would I ever consider being an art dealer!

True, a fortunate few did put aside respectable sums, due to prudence in the halcyon '8os. A handful became quite rich. Usually, however, expenses rose inexorably to match profits, even in banner years when one could do no wrong. The only way I saw a dealer achieving real financial success was to carefully store away each year, in a methodical way, works of artists he respected. Through this very technique Ileana Sonnabend and her ex-husband, Leo Castelli, amassed important collections of the artists they represented over generations— now worth many millions.

2

The Formation of the RSM Collection

At the outset, I determined to have lighthearted pleasure in collecting art. I learned that dealers usually gave a discount of 10 percent or 15 percent automatically from "list" price but, in reality, there was no list.* Confronted with shrewd businessmen as customers, they mostly wilted at the possibility of losing a sale. After consummation of the transaction, invoices called for payment within thirty days, a matter blithely ignored by wealthy clients, who paid at leisure.

*New York's Truth-in-Pricing Law (Section 20-708) now calls for a dealer to display a price list prominently.

Being in a trading business, I decided immediately that it would be an unequal contest to match wits with the dealers; actually, it would ruin my fun to carry over my finely honed skills to my new hobby. Early on, the galleries learned my parameters—that I would say "yea" or "nay," but never counter-offer. Also, it meant a lot to them that I would always pay an invoice immediately upon delivery of a work of art in good condition. After a while, the dealers tantalized me frequently with attractive prices, since they knew my intention was to amass a collection that would eventually be given to a museum; this would be a way of ensuring public exposure so important to an artist's career. On no occasion did I ever bargain to reduce a price, tempting though it might have been.

Displaying Contemporary Art at the Office

The benefits of my art collecting were basically non-mercenary. The works were displayed in the RSM offices and afforded me great visual pleasure. It also gave the company a certain prestige, since we had frequent visitors (which grew to a *flood* when the collection matured), but the RSM staff appreciated what we owned only after a painful voyage of discovery. In the begin-

15

ning, I had howls of protest at the way I was squandering precious corporate assets by buying unproductive inventory.

I began decorating the office with my art in 1970, shortly after I had instigated monumental changes in the structure of RSM. After generations of a highly regimented, autocratic family hierarchy, there was now a group of teams quite open in communications, democratic and well motivated, who worked diligently for their profit-sharing bonuses. The results gratified me, as we consistently produced earnings pleasantly in seven figures.

One price I paid was having to endure the outspokenness of the employees, who without hesitation told me their feelings about how I guided their destinies. Several high-achievers deeply resented my excursion into the art world, perceiving that this could affect the "bonus pool." Although I pointed out—to no avail—that the difference to the staff annually was only approximately $100, which I would make up out of my own pocket, they envisioned a cumulative effect over the years that might impoverish the company. Perhaps the response would have been less vehement if I had

16

chosen what they considered aesthetically worthy. Certainly contemporary art did not fill the bill in their eyes.

Faced with their strident negativity, I commenced to educate my RSM associates, hoping that they would better accept my judgment in artistic matters.

Early on, I purchased five splendid etchings and aquatints by Brice Marden (*Five Plates*), which were met with derisive catcalls. His subtle, abstract markings, superbly drawn, reminded one vice-president of "hen scratches."

More cleverly, I then purchased a set of ten lithographs by Sol LeWitt, each executed by fine artists who followed his instructions as to how the lines should be drawn (*Work From Instructions*, 1971). In this case, before the prints had been delivered to the office, I held a contest which challenged employees, their families and friends to create their own versions, based on Sol's directions. (This was intended as a modest spoof, since usually employees and their families are excluded from corporate giveaways.) Sol, who once took aerial shots of Manhattan and snipped out all the museums, loved the idea, and agreed to act as judge. I offered a photograph as a prize.

17

This competition inspired a frenzy of activity and the entries poured in, inundating my office with stacks of paper. Predictably, most people had trouble following instructions, much less executing them, but the daughter of a clerk, studying at the Art Academy, won hands down and received a congratulatory note from Sol. We installed her handiwork along the wall that later displayed the prints.

Shortly afterwards, I purchased my first work by Mel Bochner from Sonnabend Gallery. A deceptively simple oil pastel on Arches paper, one of his "3-4-5" series, it interlocked a triangle, square and pentagon in a small construct, surrounded by a wide expanse of white paper (#4964 *Trine*, 1973). Henry Huss, one of our dogged salesmen, invited me to view the masterpiece with him on the first day it had been installed.

"Bob," he sneered deprecatingly, "just *what* did you pay for THAT?"

I replied sweetly, "Henry, you're not sophisticated enough to know the truth, so I won't shock you by telling." (The cost: $4,500.)

Henry: "Why, I could do the same or better on a Sunday at home!"

Bob: "Henry, I'll make you a sporting offer. If you can do what you said, I'll pay you the same amount I paid the gallery. If there is any disagreement between us, we'll have the head of Contemporary Art Center make the final judgment. I must say that if you win, you'll receive a tidy sum."

Henry spent a pretty penny on drawing paper and a set of oil sticks, after foolishly broadcasting to his associates the deal that he and I had struck. For weeks he suffered ribbing about the "masterpiece" he was to produce, but the Sunday painting was not forthcoming. After two months, crestfallen, he came to me, admitted defeat, and deigned to acknowledge newfound respect for Mel Bochner.

Many of the artists whose work I purchased were subjects of monographs. Rarely prestigious coffee-table items, they could still be rather impressive to the uninitiated. I liked the funkier ones best and many of those were published and/or sold by Printed Matter, a storefront bookstore on Lipsenard Street, just below Canal Street in Tribeca. I started methodically buying these attractive issues and today must have at least five hundred. Ed Ruscha and Sol produced a slew of seductive material, all of which I own. Few of them originally cost more than a few dollars apiece.

Unobtrusively, I started strewing these publications around the office, especially on a table in the RSM visitors' waiting room. Employees would pick them up to peruse or take home to study, afterwards commenting with awe that there were BOOKS published about OUR artists. Somehow these printed pages validated the worth of the artists that our people had previously ignored with disdain. Few had ever taken the trouble to view what was displayed in the office, or to try to understand what I was doing. Obviously, the fact that someone considered an artist important enough to justify an entire book heightened appreciation!

My employees would avidly read the often inane texts by art critics to gain a "deeper appreciation" of our art. The same was true when I clipped reviews from the *New York Times* and put them on our company bulletin board. Our people seemed to have an insatiable appetite for the written word, and only by that method did they evince even minimal interest in the art itself. I would wonder if that phenomenon might have wider implications for the public at large. In sum, there was minimal or no recognition of the intrinsic merit of a work of art unless validated by experts writing about it.

Over time, the staff became accustomed to the growing quantity in our spacious quarters. To their surprise, they found themselves actually *missing* works when they went on loan to various museum shows and, of course, it was a point of pride that anyone would select our examples. Several times there were "Selections from the RSM Collection" at various Midwest public spaces, and RSM people would travel to Indiana or Ohio destinations to see how our works were displayed. These events served as a mysterious catalyst, creating a new positive identity for RSM.

Still, more crises would arise with regularity over the art I selected. A case in point was a work by Jenny Holzer. For some years a useful source of new young artists was the Whitney Biennial show, which—especially in the 1970s—would be on the cutting edge, providing me with names I had never known. In 1982 two youngsters caught my attention: Jenny Holzer and Barbara Kruger, who are today well-regarded, established artists. Kruger started showing immediately at the Annina Nosei Gallery on Prince Street and I purchased a large, vivid and sardonic photomontage on that trip (#2070 *Untitled*, 1978).

Holzer didn't seem to have a gallery in New York, but a couple of months later I found her work being shown at Nicholas Logsdail's Lisson Gallery in London. One particular piece captivated me. There was a succinct message painted in two lines with silver three-inch letters on thick brown wrapping paper: *WHO WAS YOUR MOTHER THAT YOU ACT SO BAD?* I paid Nicholas the princely sum of $60, wrapped my treasure in a roll and anchored it with a rubber band.

At the time I was living in La Jolla, but I continued to curate RSM's Cincinnati collection. I proudly installed the work on a wall of the office. To my consternation, a storm of protest descended as our staff considered her opus the statement of a sexist male. They found it so offensive that they didn't hear my plaintive plea that it had been done by a rather outspoken, aggressive female. Deeply aggrieved by the furor, I took it down and installed it in my loft on Greene Street in Soho.

Later, in 1988, the saga continued: I mentioned my

fiasco to Hugh Davies, director of the La Jolla Museum of Contemporary Art, and he begged me to give it to his institution, so I brought Holzer's chef d'ouevre to California and it was installed with all due honors. *

After a couple of weeks, on a random visit I noticed "Jenny" was missing and queried a friendly guard about its fate. He paled considerably and whispered: "You haven't heard?" It seemed that someone had defaced the "Holzer" with a wide felt marker-pen, writing in large, red letters: "This is art? You must be kidding!" Considering that on any given day there are more guards than visitors in the museum, it was quite an outstanding feat of vandalism.

Evidently Hugh Davies was reluctant to confess to me the fate of my major gift, but I boldly confronted him about the tragedy. Our first option was to leave the red lettering intact and have it as part of the piece. (Mistakenly, I thought it added a touch of humor.) The second choice would be to throw it in the wastebasket and

---

* Recently I received a copy of a letter sent to the La Jolla Museum from a child who had visited while on a school field trip. It said: "Thank you for letting us come to your museum. My favorite was the poster board painted with gold letters that said '*Who was your mother that you act so bad?*' that was my favorite. From that I learned that not all art is neat and clean. I would recommend anyone to go there."

forget about it. Alas, museum directors are made of sterner stuff, and Davies would not relent so easily. I learned that the museum had adequate insurance to cover such damage and, considering that MY Jenny Holzer was an early and important work, it would be fully restored.

And that is just what happened: "Jenny" has been fully restored after several years of dedicated toil and is currently displayed in one of the galleries. The skill employed to repair it was incredible: a close examination does not reveal a trace of damage. I shudder to think of the thousands of dollars expended on what originally cost $60!

A few years prior to the Jenny Holzer episode, in 1980 an event occurred that stirred up lots of negative feelings at RSM. It pertained to a large work by Gilbert and George, an inseparable homosexual couple; each small in stature and impassive of mien, they caricatured the proper Englishman by their behavior. Originally "performance" artists, they became noted for large photographic montages, usually consisting of sixteen elements, each 60 × 50 cm in size, individually framed with a narrow black metal strip—all joined together to

produce a striking image. Often they posed in outland-
ish positions, staring with their usual deadpan expres-
sion; at times they used nubile young boys as subjects,
causing a degree of outrage from an intolerant public.

I had been following their career for some ten years,
but had never bought a "Gilbert and George," since I
had higher priorities on my list. But one day I found
myself browsing Soho with the president of RSM, Bill
Jamison, who wanted me to better educate him about
the contemporary art scene. We visited the Sonnabend
Gallery to view a new show of G and G's work—which,
by coincidence, opened that day. The two masters,
whom I knew slightly, were present and they seemed
delighted when I chose a work for our collection. Indeed, Gilbert managed the vestige of a smile as he contemplated an office displaying the image I selected:
Both in profile, Gilbert, on the left, with mouth wide
open, faced George, who had his tongue stuck out quite
close to his partner's face. A quite compelling sight!

Bill was disconcerted by my decision and protested
that he and the staff would have to live with this mon-
strosity, while I dwelt at a comfortable distance in California. Scarcely listening to my cogent explanation as
to the artistic merits of the work and the importance of

the artists (actually, their fame came later), Bill adamantly opposed my judgment.

As a compromise, we finally agreed to conduct a poll of the RSM personnel as to whether the Gilbert and George should be brought to Cincinnati. I asked Antonio Homem, Sonnabend's director, to keep the work "on hold" and he gave me a couple of transparencies for the staff to view.

I was absent when Bill Jamison conducted his survey, but I have little doubt that he slanted it in his favor. Not surprisingly, the response proved overwhelmingly negative. He sent me a list of the answers, which ranged from "repulsive" to "I wouldn't work in a place that showed such degenerate rot." So, sadly, I renounced my number-one choice and purchased a tamer photographic piece (*Flying Devils*, 1980). The Baltimore Museum bought the rejected item the moment I let it go.

A year later Gilbert ànd George had a blockbuster retrospective in London. For the occasion a large, sumptuous book was published, containing examples of their work over twenty years. Appearing on the cover was the very piece that we had refused to buy (*HELL-ISH*, 1980); gleefully, I bought a couple of copies of the book, which I strategically placed in the RSM offices. After that I noticed a more docile acceptance of my preferences!

That same year, 1980, four Italian painters burst upon the New York art world, causing a major sensation. I studiously avoided Sandro Chia, since I disliked his work. (The major collector, Saatchi, bought Chias by the dozen, only later to dump them back on the market and well-nigh wreck his career.) Enzo Cucchi demonstrated great talent, but somehow I failed to buy anything of his; however, I did acquire from Marian Goodman Gallery a wonderful painting (*Alla Sicilia*, 1980) and a charming drawing of a woman's head (*Untitled*, 1980), both by Mimmo Palladino.

The fourth Italian was a remarkable genius—Francesco Clemente, one of the great draftsmen and painters of our time. His debut at Sperone Westwater Gallery was something less than a success, but Angela Westwater had little trouble in persuading me to buy an outstanding oil and encaustic on canvas (*Two Skulls*, 1980). The artist seems to have a macabre sense of self-loathing, since he constantly produces self-

27

portraits that are twisted and distended into grotesque shapes occasionally reminding me of Francis Bacon. *Two Skulls*, on a sickly yellow ground, portrays a wan self-image, with sunken cheekbones and brooding eyes, atop which is perched a skull—obviously a second Clemente.

I installed this exceptional painting proudly behind one secretary's desk. Not many days passed until she came to me and said she couldn't work properly with Clemente glowering behind her back, so I quietly moved the offending object. Before long I received a similar complaint from a clerk, who claimed the painting emitted an evil aura—I had a minor revolt on my hands. The boss, Bill Jamison, and I conducted an emergency conference about the problem; the only reasonable solution was to relegate Clemente to the "computer room," which was devoid of personnel.

The following year, 1981, I had occasion for the first time to visit the Edward Thorp Gallery on West Broadway (space now occupied by Mary Boone Gallery). My close friend Douglas Huebler (an acclaimed conceptual artist) was then dean at Cal-Arts, the famous school originally funded by Walt Disney. Doug had a coterie of brilliant students he was nurturing, and a favorite was Eric Fischl, who was about to have his first New York show with Ed Thorp. I dropped by at Doug's suggestion.

I was greeted cordially by the owner—a tall, agreeable chap, who ushered me to the rear room of his rather small quarters, where I found a group of amazing paintings lined around the walls. The vibrancy of the work entranced me, as my eye darted from one to the other. Thorp obviously recognized that he had an important discovery on his hands and he claimed to be aiming each of the works at public institutions rather than individuals. However, as I was the first visitor to see Fischl's work, he would be willing to sell me one, particularly after I explained that I would eventually donate it to a museum. They were all so dazzling I couldn't make up my mind, and I really wished to have two. One was a beach scene, with bathers romping in the sand (it's now at the Whitney Museum); the other showed a man holding a drowned, androgynous youngster in his arms at shore's edge (*Grief*, 1981; 54″×66″). Thorp limited me to one only, so I chose the latter, since it was such a compelling, tragic portrait.

I felt daring and a bit foolish, paying $4,500 for the

29

work of an unknown artist, but less than ten years later, after being displayed in museums around the world, *Grief* was appraised for a bit less than $1,000,000!

Once more I came to my *own* grief by hanging Eric Fischl's work at our office. The staff found the depiction so depressing that no one wanted that great painting nearby. As a result, to universal acclaim, it was relegated to the mail room, where it would only be seen by Dick Cox, who was in charge of our sample/mail department. Dick and our telephone operator, Helen Dahling, were my lone stalwart supporters. They appreciated everything. When visitors came to view the collection, Helen would take them on a personally guided, informative tour, leaving the switchboard lit up like a Christmas tree while our executives fumed helplessly.

Little of what RSM had in art might fall under the rubric "pleasant." Much of it violated the norms our employees considered acceptable, although usually they tolerated my whims. As example, I purchased from Sperone Westwater a "date" painting of On Kawara (*March 21, 1975* {*From Today*}). This act alone singled me out as an important collector, as having an "On Kawara" was the ultimate chic. For years he poured out this genre, always signifying the current date, sometimes containing a comma, at other times a period. They did vary at times in color and dimension and mine, at 8″ × 10″, was rather small (but not the price: $3,200). It was #18, Liquitex on canvas. It displaced a calendar on a narrow wall in front of a typist.

A few years later, On Kawara wrote and asked us to send him a photograph of where the painting was situated in the office. We obliged and he must have been delighted, for a photo of *March 21, 1975* at RSM appeared on the back cover of a hefty tome, which compiled his life's work. The RSM staff was pleased to receive such recognition.

I don't know if On Kawara still grinds out his "date" paintings, but I do know that his prices at auction have been phenomenal.

In 1978 I bought a colorful work by Jennifer Bartlett from Paula Cooper Gallery—by mistake. Entitled *Graceland Mansions*, there were five renditions of a house, all beautifully framed together: drypoint, aquatint, silkscreen, woodcut and lithograph (later swapped to the Getty Museum). Upon its arrival in

31

Cincinnati, the RSM employees fought like tigers to co-opt it and have it near them. To the resentment of many, our controller exercised his authority, hanging it in his private office. That was the only time I can remember a work of art engendering any real enthusiasm at RSM!

In my personal office I had an Adirondack chair made of plywood and covered with a bright yellow Bakelite (*Formica Lawn Chair*, 1979). It was a signature piece of Scott Burton, later shown widely at the Whitney Museum, in Canada and Europe. I placed it at the end of a long conference table and, although it was quite comfortable, no one would ever sit in it. People must have considered it sacrilegious to place their derrières on a work of art, because they recoiled when I beckoned them to be seated there.

Another fixture in my office was a "sculpture" by Carl Andre, another icon of the then-current scene. Early on, I recognized his importance and, in 1976, gathered the courage to buy a work from his dealer and close personal friend, Angela Westwater. Patiently, she explained that his steel plates, which comprised a floor piece, were sold by the unit. In other words, if I wanted a good-sized square work, consisting of 8′ × 8′ or 9′ × 9′ individual squares, all I had to do was multiply the total by $600. It didn't take a mathematical genius to determine that it would far exceed my annual budget of $20,000.

But, mercifully, Angela presented a less expensive option: I could buy rectangular—rather rusty—steel plates to be placed in a row. Each masterpiece consisted of an indivisible number, according to my predilection (i.e., 7, 11, 17, or 19), at a cost of only $400 apiece! Not wishing to appear too much of a Midwestern bumpkin, I opted for an "11" and, in my innocence, asked to be shown one I might select. At that Angela took me to a small storeroom in the rear of the gallery, where many boxes contained rusty steel plates sticking on end and separated by wooden dividers. With exemplary politeness, she said, "Here they are. You can help yourself and select your own eleven plates." So down I went, on my hands and knees, to extract a quantity of plates for a layout on the gallery floor. It actually was quite a lot of fun, feeling creative rejecting and replacing elements to come up with a suitable gestalt.

In Cincinnati I placed the eleven plates in a row, just inside the threshold of my office, forcing anyone entering to tread upon them. I would watch with amusement the contortions of those who tried to avoid stepping on and defiling my masterwork.

33

Several years later, Carl Andre received a commission to make a temporary sculpture on an overhead walkway that girds downtown Cincinnati. Consisting of untreated railroad ties, it was both well executed and positively viewed by the public.

In time I had become friendly with Angela Westwater (a native of nearby Columbus, Ohio) who requested that I give a dinner in honor of Carl after his dedication ceremony. Glad to oblige, I invited important local art world luminaries to my house and Angela flew in from New York for the grand opening.

Carl Andre appeared at my home in coveralls, looking his usual scruffy self, with luncheon crumbs still entangled in his full beard. During a superb meal, he grumbled constantly about the quality of the food: The meat was undercooked, the salad greens were limp. Later he complained that the Napoleon Cognac was inferior to what he normally drank. In the interest of amity and hospitality, I gritted my teeth and bore the indignities.

That evening I spoke with Angela and Carl about the possibility of his making an outdoor sculpture for my garden, a project I had long considered but had never instigated. They came by the next morning to survey and to probe the potential. Carl stalked our three acres alone as Angela and I gossiped together in the house. Finally he returned to announce that there would be only *one* site that he would consider for an Andre sculpture: He had selected the *middle* of my tennis court!

Utterly disgusted with his flippant effrontery, I bade a hearty farewell to Carl Andre, never to see him again.

Soon after the negative response to my purchase of works by Brice Marden and Mel Bochner, I bought a fine painting by the great minimalist John McLaughlin, who had died a few years earlier. Max Protetch, with whom I would do a lot of business, acquired it for me from Nick Wilder, the artist's great friend who had shown his work on the West Coast, and I was elated to get it (*Untitled*, 1962; 81.20 × 121.9 cm).

In 1974, Angela Westwater found me a fine work by Donald Judd, whom I had identified as being of prime importance as a minimalist. I dearly wanted a work of his at a price I could afford—not an easy task—but, true to her name, that Angel located one, which took care of *that* year's budget (*Untitled*, 1974; anodized green aluminum; 12.7 × 101.6 × 21.6 cm). It looked spectacular on the wall leading to my personal office.

Next, I bought an impressive oil painting by Elizabeth Murray from her first show at Paula Cooper's

(*Rolling Ball*, 1975; 151.8 × 152.7 cm). It stands out in my mind today as being very special; its vibrant colors, divided so intelligently, bring a smile as I visualize it in my mind. Since then Elizabeth Murray has grown and changed, always producing spectacular, challenging work.

That same year I bought from Marian Goodman a fanciful "sculpture" by Robert Wilson—a miniature straight-backed chair made of wire mesh. I have lost the dimensions, because no sooner had I acquired it than Bob Stearns grabbed it for the CAC. He installed it directly above the entrance to the gallery, where it twists enchantingly in a breeze formed each time the door opens. It has a good home and a lot of public exposure.*

Art dealers are notoriously sloppy in how they make their sales and seem unaware of what, in other fields, might be considered grievous business practices. Due to poor liaison by the staff, it is not uncommon for a

---

*I must have a penchant for wire mesh sculpture, because most recently, in 1993, I bought a lovely, small, painted "box" of the same material, by Lucas Samaras at a Christie's auction. It had been owned by Saatchi and I bought it for 15 percent of what he had paid Pace Gallery some years earlier. It now rests on a ledge in my living room.

sale of the same object to be made almost simultaneously to two different people and probably at two different prices. Of course, this can cause incredible distress to a serious collector. The words "hold" and "option" have little meaning except to the prospective buyer, who may want a reasonable period of time to make a decision or to talk it over with a spouse. Commercial terminology has little significance when it comes to buying art. Recognizing this, I made up my mind never to get upset, even if I received a flagrant double-cross, since there was art being made every day and if I didn't buy one thing, there was plenty left to choose.

I was rather unique in my attitude and I suffered at the hands of dealers rather frequently, because they knew I would respond mildly to cavalier treatment. Normally I stayed well clear of those high demand, limited supply situations, if only because the price might be well out of reach.

The year 1976 brought me both failures and successes in my acquisitive art efforts. Two episodes occurred in which I came out a loser.

The first involved Paula Cooper, an alluring, gracious lady, of whom I had become enormously fond.

With her usual loyalty and tenacity, Paula promoted the career of a young artist, Jennifer Bartlett, who produced wonderful, colorful art in a variety of media. I had bought several works on paper and looked for something more substantial. Along one wall at Bartlett's new show was an astounding piece: She had painted a series of images, primarily houses, on eighty baked enamel plates, which formed a single work of art $57'' \times 259''$—in other words, over twenty feet long and almost six feet high (*Falcon Avenue*, 1976)! I could immediately visualize it placed along a wall, just to the left as one entered our office. Paula was delighted at my interest, since the work obviously wouldn't fit in many living rooms, but she said that the Whitney Museum had had a hold on it for some time, with the option to expire the following Friday. Since the price was reasonable and within my budgetary constraints, I told her that I would purchase *Falcon Avenue* if the option lapsed.

Losing my usual aplomb, I was on pins and needles until the great day arrived, since I felt it would be a coup to obtain such a special item. Just before Paula Cooper closed on Friday, she confirmed to me that the Whitney had *not* responded and that the treasure was mine. That weekend I glowed with pleasure at my good fortune; it was the first time I had acquired something I REALLY wanted.

The next Tuesday, at home after work, I sat perusing the latest edition of *New York Magazine*. As I thumbed through it in desultory fashion, my eye caught a feature story about Jennifer Bartlett. Opposite to the article was a full-page reproduction of *Falcon Avenue*! I rushed to show everyone in the household this incredible coincidence, feeling quite puffed up over the matter. What an eye I had for great art!

The next Wednesday morning I received a telephone call from Paula Cooper: "Bob, the Whitney just called and accepted the Jennifer Bartlett. I'm sorry." I responded with all the technical arguments I could summon, arguing eloquently the justice of my position with my usual persuasiveness, all to no avail. Paula responded with commendable candor: "Bob, if it is a choice between you and the Whitney, the Whitney wins." Sadly, I could understand her position and just how important it was for Jennifer Bartlett's career, so I bowed out with good grace.

On my next trip East I went to John Weber Gallery to view a new show of Sol LeWitt, hoping to acquire a major work. It was a wonderful display of about sixteen white constructs, each of which consisted of nine hollow squares in various combinations, all beautifully crafted. It followed a series of variations on a single large cube that had been produced several years earlier. Most of what I saw were rather large floor pieces, unsuitable for our office, but there were two stunning wall pieces, and I selected one for RSM.

Because of the size, I had a gnawing feeling that the element might not fit into our freight elevator, so I obtained an option on the piece until I could go to Cincinnati and check the exact elevator dimensions. John Weber and his director, Amy Baker, couldn't have been more cooperative and understanding.

When I returned home, the building manager and I measured carefully and, after recalculating several times, we concluded that Sol's piece was slightly too wide—ironically, just by a few millimeters. So I phoned Amy to tell her the bad news, saying that I would give a final answer within a week, since I was examining other possibilities.

In fact, the solution I found was quite simple—to me, that is, but to no one else: We could have a blow torch remove a few casement windows with ease, which would afford adequate entry space. Then we'd hire a giant crane that would lift "Sol" to our ninth-floor office, after which a welder could reseal the windows. Of course, we would need a city permit for the operation, but the crane would operate late at night, since our offices in the Gwynn Building were on Sixth Street, a main thoroughfare in downtown Cincinnati. Like magic our problem would be solved!

Planning the specific logistics took a few days, after which I called Amy Baker with my glad tidings; but she informed me that John Weber had become impatient at the delay in my answer and had sold MY sculpture to the Weatherspoon Gallery in Greensboro, North Carolina! With all my ingenuity gone to waste, I felt rather crestfallen to have missed such a significant creation. Yet I brightened considerably when Amy told me that Sol had been incensed at John's inexcusable act and was having a special piece constructed for me, with dimensions that would allow ingress on the elevator. It would be ready upon my return and I could have it if it met

41

with my approval. Thrilled at Sol's gentlemanly response, I could scarcely wait to see what the new work looked like.

A few months later, I found myself on lower Broadway at the second-floor studio where Sol's work was made. He had three Japanese master craftsmen—the Watanabe brothers and Kazuko-san, a fine artist in her own right—build all pieces according to his instructions.

Kazuko-san (who later became a friend) showed me two double-sized works, each incredibly wonderful. Taking both was out of the question, so I spent a whole hour anguishing over which one to choose. The one I selected was roughly in the shape of a "T" with three equidistant "arms." The horizontal arms, full width, were actually seventeen hollow squares across, eight on each side of a central square. From the latter square, the vertical part of the "T" extended downward eight more squares. At the focal center square, the construct was nine squares deep, the three abutting it were eight squares deep, the next squares seven deep, and so on, until at the end of each arm, there was just one solitary square.

The effect was magical, offering the illusion that a

giant, winged bird was poised to take flight from the wall. I was staggered by LeWitt's ability to visualize a great masterpiece by merely jotting down instructions. By all odds, it remains my favorite purchase of all, and for years rested on the wall just behind Helen, the telephone operator—the first item viewed in the office: *Wall Piece #8203* (1976).

The story has another twist: When we unwrapped *#8203* upon arrival at our office, I noticed that at least one coat of paint was missing from perhaps six squares at the tip of the righthand wing. The whole work looked as though it had been covered with white enamel, except for this minor oversight. I had no idea how many coats had been applied originally, or how many were still needed for the defective spot.

I telephoned Amy Baker to explain the problem and offered to pay the cost of Kazuko-san's flight to Cincinnati so that she could make the necessary adjustment. She assured me the matter would be dealt with expeditiously. A few days went by without a response, but one morning I received a small parcel via Federal Express. I unwrapped the package and found therein a small can of paint and a brush! Since the message was quite clear, that Saturday, quivering in terror, I applied

43

the paint to the offending areas—without mishap, but I was always left with the feeling that for $7,000 I could have had *slightly* more personal attention! Yet stronger was my gratitude to Sol for his magnanimity in providing me with a double-sized piece for the same money I was originally quoted.

In 1970 I had visited the country home of Amy and Joe Pulitzer in St. Louis. She had been curator at the local museum for many years and the two of them had built a remarkable collection. For the first time I viewed the work of young Richard Serra, who had divided their lawn with a series of steel plates, partially buried in the sod. It made a lasting impression and I resolved to own something of his.

Some years later, Cora Rosevear took me to a Serra show, which displayed his "lead" pieces for the first time. Each consisted of a heavy lead plate, balanced precariously on a lead rod against a wall or in the corner of the room, which made them appear threatening, even dangerous (a precursor to his giant steel plates, which *did* collapse in a Greene Street gallery, killing a workman and causing the building to be closed for extended repairs). The price of $5,000 was reasonable, but since I couldn't visualize a suitable spot in our office, I passed up a great opportunity. As a poor consolation I bought a fine lithograph 52.25″ × 41.25″ (*Du Common*, 1972).

Equally frustrating was my inability to buy a sculpture of Richard Long, an outstanding English artist. Marian Goodman (not his regular dealer) offered me a great floor piece available for resale at $5,500. It consisted of various hewn granite rocks of random sizes, all of the same height, that formed an eight-foot circle. I panted to have it, but where in the world would I have put it?

Not much later I did acquire a great photograph, taken on one of his long journeys on foot. Sperone Westwater had an exhibit of his photos, all priced at $4,000 or $5,000. Angela introduced me to Richard Long, a tall, lanky gentleman; I told him how much I respected his artistry in such a range of media. I confided to him my "modus operandi" in behalf of my local museum and that, besides painting and sculpture, I was buying "conceptual" photography; however, I had a limitation of $2,000 to purchase an individual photo (which, in my naiveté, I thought was a considerable sum of money). He seemed interested in my project and

45

politely muttered something to the effect that I might hear from him sometime.

Six months passed and one day I had a phone call from Angela Westwater: "Bob, Richard Long has sent on something for you that I'll hold until you're in town." It turned out that the "something" was a great photograph, entitled *A Circle in Africa: Mulanje Mountain Malawi* (1978; 34.5″×48.5″). Enclosed with it was a note, penned with wry humor: "I managed to meet your price limitation, since the 'Circle' has had much adverse publicity." Accompanying his missive was a catalogue of his recent one-man show at the Stedlijk Museum in Amsterdam, on the cover of which was the "Circle." It remains the most gracious act during the many years I collected art, and I was very appreciative. Today it remains my favorite photo.

Paula Cooper was always so supportive of artists, even those she could not represent regularly, that she'd display a single painting to help a struggling career. One day I saw a compelling oil by Robert Moskowitz, who she said was moonlighting as a taxi driver to make ends meet. In his work, a mysterious figure, possibly drowning, was represented by a single arm shown just above the elbow and bent so that the limb and hand were parallel to a body of water, quite possibly the ocean. I was transfixed by this haunting image and was determined to have it; furthermore, the price was more than reasonable. But something distracted my attention—perhaps a friend appeared, who engaged me in conversation—so I left the gallery without informing Paula of my intention.

Two days later I dropped by to confirm the purchase, only to find the painting missing. It seemed that Jennifer Bartlett had been similarly entranced and had traded Moskowitz one of her works for his! Much later I saw the "Moskowitz" at MOMA, which had received it as a gift. It was to be the only instance when I deeply regretted having been stupidly inattentive.

Some years later I bought a stunning "architectural" painting (*Untitled*, 1966–70; 28.25" × 48.5") and a small Robert Moskowitz drawing from Daniel Weinberg Gallery in San Francisco, but they lacked the incredible emotional impact of "the one that got away." I gave *Untitled* to the Oakland Museum; the drawing hangs in my bathroom.

47

My second debacle was more pecuniary than aesthetic, although it involved a great painting: Marian Goodman and I ambled about her gallery one day and she analyzed the special aura of Anselm Kiefer's brooding landscapes. It was his first show and she puzzled over the tepid reaction of the public. As we perused some incredible "books" he had made, in walked Morton Neumann, the preeminent American collector of contemporary art whose holdings were exhibited in consecutive years at the National Gallery.

Mort joined our conversation and uncharacteristically seemed undecided about Kiefer's work. He asked my opinion and, flattered, I responded that Kiefer must be one of the most important artists of the twentieth century. All of the paintings were gigantic in size except one, which was about four and a half feet square—a manageable dimension—and was a beauty. I urged Mort to buy it, that if he didn't, I would. (I was then a consultant to Marian and felt my self-effacing stance was correct.) After hemming and hawing, he decided to pass (a decision he later regretted), so I told Marian that I would take it gladly.

When I returned to Cincinnati, I found an invoice had already arrived—in the amount of $7,000, as she

48

had quoted, but the usual 10 percent discount was missing. I called New York to point out this oversight and Marian replied that the work was so unique and reasonably priced that she wouldn't cede a nickel. So we had a clash of wills and I informed her haughtily that under those circumstances I wouldn't buy the painting if she remained so obdurate. The result: Within days she sold it elsewhere.

Within a handful of years Anselm Kiefer became the most renowned living artist in the world and I could have sold the work easily for a hundred times my cost.

Later, as a poor substitute, I did buy a trivial work of Kiefer. It was one of a series of gouaches, painted on a photograph with a few broad, gestural strokes. On each he had affixed strands of straw, and across the top had scrawled in German, "Golden-Haired Margaret." Mine had a shot of a staircase, rather indistinct and un-inspiring (*Dein Goldenes Haar Margarete*, 1981–82; gelatin silver print, gouache and straw; 58.6×83.2 cm). For this mediocrity, in a fit of madness I paid $3,000.

For a long time this Kiefer work hung in my front hall, a constant reproach for my earlier pigheadedness. I heartily disliked the work. Not only did it remind me of my pigheadedness, but also the straw started becoming unstuck and sunlight seemed to be degrading it.

In the late '80s New York dealer Jack Tilton paid me a visit. I had become a friend when he worked for Betty Parsons, a legendary figure for generations, who bequeathed her business to Jack at her death. He had fine contacts and did a lot of "back room" profitable deals in art resales other than what he normally handled. He spotted my "Kiefer" and said it was worth a fortune! If he could take a transparency back home, he felt he could pay me $125,000 and make a reasonable profit himself. I could scarcely believe what he told me; I knew the art market was wild and here was a specific example. To my vast relief the sale went through and I had disposed of an unwanted object. A few years later, in late 1993, I saw a similar work of Kiefer in a Christie's fall catalogue. The estimated price: $15,000.

After Jack bought the Kiefer, I sold several other works, with the proceeds designated for a scholarship fund I've established for minority students. In that crazy, frenzied period, it was the only time I ever sold anything. The opportunity to vend artwork had been irresistible and I found myself uncomfortable having such expensive art in my home.

3

Dealers and Artists

During several decades, I have gotten to know dozens of dealers throughout the United States and western Europe—some slightly, and a handful quite well. I never became an intimate friend of a dealer, although with several I established a relationship of affection and mutual respect.

Each gallery exudes its own unique personality the moment a stranger crosses the threshold. A subtle message emanates at the entrance. Having been a practicing psychologist, specializing in communications, I receive signals rapidly. They range from "Please come in and look around. May we help you?" to "We are available only to important customers. Make your stay as brief as possible."

Of course, dealers know that rarely does an unknown person walk in off the street and make a significant purchase, so the odds are that they would fritter away their time by answering inane questions posed by ignoramuses. To combat intrusions, they construct barriers such as closed doors or velvet ropes that cordon off the office areas. At times in the main gallery area there is no live body, but more often an amanuensis is seated behind a counter, fending off enquiries and protecting the important personages concealed in the rear.

Some of the most prestigious galleries are so forbidding that even I dread entering them. If that is the reaction of a *poised* buyer, I can imagine how cowed other less experienced, incipient collectors must feel. Often these places have outstanding shows. Recently Gagosian Gallery had a series of exhibitions that would do any museum proud. Seemingly they were aimed at his select clientele, Michael Ovitz, Doug Cramer, or Si Newhouse, who can and will pay more for a single painting than I will spend cumulatively in a lifetime.

We others share an enthusiasm for buying art along

with the titans. Some rarefied operations do miss sales to those of us who wouldn't dream of subjecting ourselves to abject groveling in order to spend money. Occasionally I've sent a dealer friend as emissary to buy in my behalf. A dealer will get a far deeper discount, so it delights me that a decent person can get in the middle and reap a pleasant profit.

On my special list are Knoedler, Marlborough, Mary Boone, Gagosian—and Pace Galleries, where my friend Doug Baxter is now uptown gallery director. He claims that my cowardly defensiveness is totally unwarranted, as Pace is a warm, yummy place; yet I see evidence to the contrary as I have escalated my visits there. I do hold myself erect, with head high, as I page Doug upon arrival, but I could sure do without the cold, fishy stare from the receptionist.

I have never known anyone at these other galleries I mentioned except for Mary Boone, whom I once briefly met. A friend had given me the name of Malcolm Morley, an English painter, whose work he thought I should consider. Mary Boone had opened her shop not long before and represented Morley, so when I came to discuss the matter, she graciously agreed to receive me.

As I explained my mission, she tapped a writing instrument impatiently on the table and informed me curtly that his work was *so* in demand that there was a waiting list for his paintings. She had quite a few people ahead of me, but she'd be glad to add my name and when my turn came up, she'd let me know. When she turned her head I knew with certainty I had been dismissed. Shell-shocked, I staggered to the street.

I didn't blame her for dispensing with introductory pleasantries when we met, but there was no chance for me to even view Morley's work, or discuss the size, content and price of what I might be buying. Others accepted gratefully what she assigned to them "when their turn came up."

Early this year I went back to see Mary Boone, although I should have known better. My mission was just the reverse of the previous encounter: I had a "Malcolm Morley" to *sell*. Three years before, at the height of the crazy art market, a friend, who is a struggling dealer, had persuaded me to finance the purchase of a Morley "ship painting," dating from the late '6os. He had acquired it from the painter's ex-wife and could easily obtain triple the amount in resale. Since the cost was just shy of $30,000, this would be quite a coup! I would receive a share of the profit—money I neither needed nor wanted—but I agreed to assist.

It seemed quite logical to me that Mary Boone was the perfect candidate for disposing of the work. Armed with a transparency of the work, I entered her gallery, hoping to obtain an audience with the owner. At a desk to the rear of the gallery, a polite lady informed me that it would be patently impossible to meet with Mary Boone, who, in fact, had no spare time for appointments for weeks to come. I explained the purpose of my call, but before I could give specific details the woman turned her attention to another visitor. Meekly, I requested a paper and pencil and jotted down my name, telephone number and address, then interrupted her conversation to beg that someone call me regarding the matter. Of course I heard nothing.

My dealer friend's timing, as it turned out, couldn't have been worse—as the market collapse had begun. I got stuck with a painting of a steamboat, which I didn't like or want to own. All efforts to dispose of it have failed, even though I would readily take a loss. Despite the fact that Malcolm Morley has had several blockbluster shows lately and had glowing press reviews, not a nibble has been forthcoming. The piece is at the Beaubourg in Paris in a big exhibit of his work, awaiting that perceptive customer who must exist *somewhere*.

Having eviscerated my bête noires, I can report that most contacts with vendors have been pleasurable. I found the works of wonderful artists in England, France, Spain, Germany and Italian galleries, and always wondered why there wasn't more cross-fertilization.

In London, both Nicholas Logsdail (Lisson Gallery) and Nigel Greenwood (whose gallery is now defunct) have had strong American affiliations, which assured their artists exposure in the U.S. market. Each taught me a lot, and frequently I have bought at low prices, particularly when the dollar was strong.

In Paris many competent dealers showed the work of fine artists; in only one case were any of the paintings or sculptures shown in New York.

One day I visited the Galerie Crousel-Hussenot. In a debut exhibit, they displayed the work of José María Sicilia, obviously a man with a fine career ahead of him. The paintings were all first-rate and I was implored to buy one so he could have a sale in America listed on his curriculum vitae. For $950 (delivered to Cincinnati) I

56

bought a large painting (*Ponceuse*, 1983; oil on canvas; 259.1 × 189.5 cm). The image of a large cannon, outlined in red, with white and blue background, is quite arresting.

The following year Blum Helman Gallery in New York gave Sicilia a show. Today he has fame and commands lofty prices.

In Paris I also bought fanciful works on paper by Annette Messager, who has shown at Holly Solomon Gallery, and from Crousel-Hussenot an artist I liked even better: François Boué.

Like my children, I could tell that Boué had been teethed on the entrancing "comic" books of "Tintin," and his daring global adventures whose author, Hergé, had recently died, sending much of Europe into mourning. In commemoration of this sad event, Boué had painted a two-part tribute, with the enigmatic title *Tim's Grab* (1983–84; 205 × 240 cm). On the bottom section is a fiery funeral pyre, on which Tintin has been laid. The upper part portrays Tintin wafting ethereally to heaven. Millions of grieving followers could resonate with Boué's feelings, so eloquently expressed. I knew my kids would appreciate it greatly.

Only once did I succeed in interesting a New York

gallery in one of my European "finds." I had bought a few things from Metro Pictures in Soho—several Cindy Sherman photographs and a large drawing by Robert Longo—so I was not unknown there. To my infinite pleasure, at my suggestion they gave a show of Werner Büttner's work, which I believe did very well. I had bought several large canvases from Max Hetzler Gallery of Cologne—*Working in Abu Dhabi* and *Cross Without Title*, both 1983—which were exceptional paintings.

Many fine paintings and sculptures that I bought in Europe over 15 years lie unappreciated and gathering dust in the bowels of the Cincinnati Art Museum. Others have been sold off for a pittance, since the staff had no inkling of what great work they owned.

Steingrim Laursen

Steingrim Laursen and I met in New York in the early '70s and our friendship ripened on my semi-annual excursions to RSM's subsidiary in Copenhagen.

Steingrim is a tall, extraordinarily handsome man, patrician in bearing, yet with a self-effacing manner. At that time he acted as an unofficial advisor to the great Louisiana Museum, organizing and curating special exhibitions. He had been accumulating a modest—but impressive—personal art collection, selected carefully from a wide range of artists he discovered as he darted around the world. In addition, he acted as a private dealer, primarily representing his close friend Jan Groth. No one could match Steingrim's perspective on the international art scene, and time and again he exposed me to the work of artists I otherwise would not have known. Jan Groth was one.

Jan Groth is another tall Adonis, whose family has a publishing empire in Norway. He has a gentle, courtly nature and I liked him immediately. He and his ex-wife, Benedikte, had been painstakingly weaving marvelous tapestries for years. All but unknown in the United States in 1974, he had made one sale in America to the immense De Menil collection.

It took forever for Jan to produce a tapestry—and the price of one was well beyond my guideline—but he was determined that I should have one. So he suggested weaving a piece smaller than normal that would be more affordable. So I became the proud owner of a great wall hanging (*Sign*, 1975–76; wool and cotton; 149.8 × 208.2 cm). Typically, it is deceptively simple: subtle white streaks wend through a dark brown background, producing an exquisite effect. It remains an all-time favorite and I would never have parted with it if I had had the wall space available in my home to properly display it.

In 1973, when I was first introduced to Jan's work, I bought four superb drawings, each containing a few stark black crayon lines on a wide expanse of thick white paper (each *Untitled*, 1973; 62.2×87.6 cm). These jewels accompanied the tapestry along with my other gifts to the Cincinnati Art Museum, who thought so little of them that they sold three of the four, beautifully framed, for a total of $30 at the infamous Chicago "auction." (I had paid $550 *apiece*, and fifteen years later his dealer, Diane Brown, sold ones quite similar for $2,000 each! In 1990 Jan Groth had an exhibit at the La Jolla Museum, where I obtained a drawing out of the show for $1,000. Jan gave me a special deal since I had contributed a modest sum to bring his work to California.)

Unflaggingly, Steingrim would widen my horizons with all kinds of incidental information that often came in handy. He introduced me to the "Cobra" school of painters, most prominent of whom were Karel Appel and Asger Jörn. Both had many examples of their work at the "Louisiana," and Jörn was so beloved in Denmark that a special museum was dedicated to his work.

In Cincinnati one evening I attended a benefit auction in behalf of the Cincinnati Contemporary Art Center. It was an annual event, called "Cincinnati Collects"—which I renamed "Cincinnati *Rejects*," since the good burghers invariably disgorged unwanted junk from their attics. Before the Sotheby's auctioneer started proceedings, I wandered about to inspect the offerings and spotted two really worthwhile specimens: one, a large, fine print by Hunterwasser, and a typical painting, $36'' \times 30''$, by Asger Jörn, full of grotesque human figures.

The auctioneer tried to stir up the competitive instincts of the crowd—but to little avail—so he quickly disposed of lot after lot. Early on, I bought the Hunterwasser for $600, a fraction of its resale value. When the Jörn painting came up, the Sotheby's fellow muttered that this was the *prize* of the event. He asked for an opening bid of $4,000 and was greeted with silence. He then kept dropping the price—finally down to $1,000, when I finally raised my hand. Somebody must have sensed that I wanted to buy it and started bidding against me to have fun. The price rose back up to $2,200, where it was knocked down to me. Later on, the auctioneer congratulated me on my purchase: "I hope you know what a rare bargain you got. If you ever want to send the Jörn painting to New York, I guarantee a profit of many times what you paid."

I took the painting home and inspected it, finding on the back of the canvas the title, *Asgarvorn*, and a penned inscription: "To my friend, Stanley Rowe, Asger Jörn." I telephoned Stanley—a fine fellow my age, the scion of an old, distinguished Cincinnati family. When queried about the painting he related this anecdote:

In the early 1950s he had been a member of a "print club," whose mentor was a fellow named Von Groschwitz, a curator of prints and drawings at the CAM, who introduced young, avid collectors to a wide variety of works on paper by artists of international repute. Prices were incredibly low, so it was an inexpensive hobby. Stanley liked a print by the Dane Asger Jörn, which the curator had brought back from Europe, so he bought it for $25.

A few months later, Stanley received a pathetic letter from Asger Jörn, intimating that he was near starvation. Since his benefactor, "Mr. Rowe," had been the first to buy his work in America, he had taken the liberty of sending on a painting, with the hope that it might be to his liking. If so, his letter suggested, please do the favor of remitting whatever amount Mr. Rowe felt it was worth. Stanley recalled that he had sent $100 to Denmark and then stored the work in a closet, where it had remained all those years, until recently, when he sent it to the CAC for the auction.

Stanley expressed astonishment that I had paid $2,200 and was even more amazed when told that Jörn had become an internationally famous name. Gracious and generous-spirited by nature, he seemed sincerely pleased at my purchase. He obliged me by digging out Jörn's original letter as well as a copy of his letter of transmittal.

When my Danish associates learned of my acquisition, they were ecstatic with joy—in fact, to such an extent that I had to bring the painting to Copenhagen to hang in the office, where it rests today, over twenty-five years later.

In the meantime, we have been badgered relentlessly by Steingrim Laursen, who wants it as a gift for his museum. As we have resisted his blandishments, he has switched tactics, promising to raise a large sum of money to buy it from us. He assesses it as a seminal work of great historical importance that doesn't belong in private hands. To partially placate him, I let him have the correspondence, which he considered a significant addition to the archives of Asger Jörn memorabilia.

I owe a debt of gratitude to Steingrim and I guess I'll have to bequeath my Asger Jörn to the Louisiana Museum.

Paula Cooper

Paula represents a constructive force along a wide spectrum of the arts. Over the years she has made her gallery space available for performances by poets, dancers and musicians, who sorely needed exposure to the public.

She knows how to twist my arm to cough up money for her pet projects, which include most of the non-profit art organizations, or assistance for those suffering from AIDS. In sum, Paula Cooper has a big heart!

I've watched her resuscitate the faltering careers of estimable artists, including Robert Mangold and Donald Judd. Some of the artists never demonstrated appreciation. In 1986, when Carl Andre, facing a criminal trial (he was later acquitted), became a pariah in the art community, Paula stuck by him valiantly as a friend and dealer. She had been representing him for six years and continues to today.

Lately Paula has reaped the bitter harvest of ingratitude, which she absorbed with incredible dignity. For more than twenty years she nurtured the career of sculptor Joel Shapiro, who became renowned internationally and a multimillionaire under her aegis. Certainly the success derived from his incredible ability, but Paula Cooper deserves major credit for her role, as she assiduously orchestrated his development each step of the way as mentor and close personal friend. Recently he abruptly left Paula Cooper's gallery for Pace Gallery, under circumstances I deem repugnant.

From the start, Cooper has always been supportive of the artists she represents with even-handedness and tenacity. Jennifer Bartlett, Elizabeth Murray and Jonathan Borofsky—just to name a few—have reached the pinnacle of success; others, just as talented, haven't had their good fortune, yet she persists in pushing their work year after year in her gallery space. For instance, Alan Shields, whom I have never met, is a wonderful painter whose work I bought eagerly. (His dappled acrylic on wood grid graced a place of honor at RSM:

Swing Dive, Low Love, 1974; 137.2 × 137.2 cm.) Also, I purchased great works on paper as well. Inexplicably, his fame has been transcended by that of other artists.

Another favorite is the well-respected Michael Hurson, a warm, likable person, whom I got to know rather well. He had painted the portraits of Paula's two sons, and she sought other commissions for him, so I readily assented for Michael to come to Cincinnati and "do" my daughter Robin and later my son Eddie (which never transpired).

Everyone in the household liked him immediately, particularly our beloved cook, Lottie, who basked in the praise he showered upon her culinary skills.

In the balmy springtime, Robin posed for Michael in the afternoons. Quickly, one impediment arose: my granddaughter, Leila, then three years old, kept crawling onto her mother's lap. Michael made the cunning suggestion that he limn the two together. Over many weeks, I watched the protracted process with fascination. Michael painted a series of drawings with pastel, conte crayon and pencil on tracing paper, each fresh one slightly more refined than the previous one. He then painted a preliminary version, and later a final one (*Portrait of Robin and Leila Sinclaire*, 1982; 63.5 × 73.1 cm).

I don't know if it was Lottie's food or Michael's relishing the loving attention lavished by my family, but he tarried so long I thought he'd become a permanent fixture; we liked him so much, we hated to see him return to New York. Robin kept the finished work and I gave the other painting and sketches to the CAM. His painting was mildly surrealistic. Robin, somewhat literal-minded, didn't at first like it, but I think that after mellowing over the years, she has grown rather fond of the portrait.

A few years later Leila visited the CAM with her kindergarten class. A condescending docent explained carefully to the children about landscapes, still-lifes, portraits, etc. "Children, do any of you know what a portrait is?" Of course, Leila piped up: "Certainly. MY portrait is hung in the next room!" The good lady was in a state of shock and disbelief.

More than ten years passed, with Michael's and my paths crossing infrequently. In the spring of 1993 Paula Cooper convinced me that I should purchase six pastel and crayon drawings, all signature works that spanned his long, fruitful career. These would form the nucleus of a show of Hurson's work at the La Jolla Museum,* sponsored by the director, Hugh Davies. These splendid items now reside in the executive offices of the museum, since I have no room for them in my home.

Another anecdote involved Robin: In 1985, when I was about to dispose of the RSM Collection, I suggested that perhaps she would like one or two works of art to retain personally. She carefully perused the computer printout, the contents of which she knew well, and decided there was nothing she really wanted; however, there was one work by Jennifer Bartlett that she "half-liked" (*In the Garden #82*, 1980; watercolor and pencil; 50.2×65.6 cm). Robin thought that the pastel on the right side was delightful, but that the far superior pencil drawing on the left half was "icky." Could I possibly find a piece that was ALL pastel?

(Bartlett had spent the summer at a villa on the French Riviera and produced 104 works, all based on the private garden there, primarily depicting a reflect-

*In 1994 the La Jolla Museum was closed for extensive renovation and expansion (a rite that seems to occur every fifteen years or so), but when it reopens, they will put on Michael Hurson's show and I will make a gift then of my recent acquisitions.

ing pool and frequently a cherub that lurked beyond. The pleasing outcome had sold like hotcakes, and Bob Stearns of the CAC and I were lucky to each acquire one. Also, the publisher Harry Abrams had printed a lavish book with photos of the entire series.)

On a New York trip, somewhat embarrassed, I told Paula about Robin's reaction and request. Good-naturedly, my friend laughed, saying that Robin was not alone. She showed me six great drawings from the "Garden" series that remained unsold. We both agreed that these were the finest of all, but only "color" seemed to sell. There were no pastels left, but Paula promised to be on the lookout for one.

Two days later she called and told me that the eminent architect Phillip Johnson had dropped by the gallery and wanted to dispose of his *In the Garden #72*, since he felt it a bit boring and had tired of it; so Robin became the proud possessor of a pastel in pale green and blues that couldn't hold a candle (in my opinion) to the one she renounced. She loves it!

A list of what I bought from Paula over the years would be long indeed. With her guidance, and that of her gallery director, Doug Baxter, I made felicitous choices, always reasonably priced and well within my budget. Sometimes their enthusiasm didn't coincide with mine. I avoided the work of Linda Benglis and Jonathan Borofsky—probably a serious error but one I don't regret. I did acquire oeuvres of most of her other artists. I admired particularly Paula's directing my attention to artists whom she did *not* represent.

One day I spotted a large, arresting painting in the back gallery. Paula said it was by a youngster named Christopher Wool, who had been Joel Shapiro's assistant for some time. Recently he had taken the plunge and had his own studio where he worked full-time. It would be a favor to her if I took the time to visit Wool and view what he was doing.

Upon arrival I found a very nervous young man with beads of perspiration as he faced a frightening ordeal with a collector. Studio visits are invariably awkward for both parties. The artist is at such a disadvantage with a prospective client. A dealer plays a significant part in leveling the field and reducing tension between artist and collector.

The work was outstanding and I greatly relished the visit, as Christopher visibly relaxed. We both felt a sense of relief and pleasure when I chose to buy *The Jury's Out*, 1984, which I had seen at Paula's.

A few days later at an opening at Artist's Space, I suddenly found myself in a bear hug with a burly man and received a moist kiss. Startled, I focused on the eminent Joel Shapiro, who expressed undying gratitude for my supportiveness of his protégé. Soon afterwards, a letter from Christopher's father, an important scientist in Chicago, expressed effusive thanks for my "good deed."

Shortly after this event, the artist's career took off and today Christopher Wool is enjoying outstanding success.

Only once can I recall that Paula's suggestion turned out poorly. A few years ago she touted a young woman named Meg Webster, an ideal candidate to do a piece for my garden. This off-beat artist followed the path of Robert Smithson (famed for his monumental *Spiral Jetty* at Salt Lake City) in creating unusual earth works.

In New York, Meg came to our Greene Street loft where we seemed to establish a strong rapport. She burst with novel ideas for a "sculptural site," scribbling sketches on a scrap of paper as we chatted. It was highly stimulating and I looked forward to a rewarding collaboration. Meg appeared quite grateful for an opportunity, since she confessed to sorely needing work. I would hear from her shortly, she said, after she crystallized some thoughts.

But that was the last I ever heard from Meg Webster. Paula was puzzled and distressed by her odd behavior and, over the next twelve months, needled her occasionally about her evident neglect. Just after our meeting, Webster's career took off and she became enormously popular, receiving commissions from wealthier, more well known collectors.

Marian Goodman

Marian Goodman is very special to me. She became my friend, and over the years we have shared many intimate feelings. Running an important gallery as a single woman (or man) can be a very lonely life and naturally, at times, one needs someone to turn to for advice and understanding—or simply to let off steam. Hopefully I've played that role to some extent.

In the field of art, there is no one I respect more than Marian. Her incredible erudition and refined taste are awe-inspiring. Her formal art history education has served her well, and she has chosen great artists to represent. Marian has a rare integrity that precludes her displaying anything in her gallery which doesn't meet her aesthetic criteria.

Like many prominent dealers, Marian has high monthly expenses, so it takes a lot of character for her to refuse showing "in" artists who are capable of bringing revenues amounting to hundreds of thousands of dollars. Her competitors do not always have such punctilious distinction.

Respected for her honor, Marian has gained a fine reputation, and represents world-class artists, primarily of European birth and domicile. In no particular order of importance, a partial list includes Rebecca Horn, Anselm Kiefer, Gerhard Richter and Ger Van Elk—as well as the Americans Dan Graham and Lawrence Weiner. In addition, she had a lively publishing business, Multiples, that produced splendid editions of Claes Oldenburg, Sol LeWitt and many others.

For a long time, trusting Marian's judgment, I acquired works for RSM and later for my garden that are truly outstanding. She no longer shows Martin Disler, Walter Dahn and Markus Lupertz, but they too af-

forded important additions. In recent years after re-
nouncing further buying, I found myself tempted by a
great landscape photograph of the area in Venezuela
historically known as "El Dorado" by Lothar Baum-
garten. As usual, Marian convinced me I should have
it!

I used to counsel my friend to keep her inventory in
bounds and keep sales moving, advice derived from my
trader's mentality. When I didn't oblige her personally,
I regretted it, but usually it was a question of inadequate floor space at the office or the price exceeding my
budget. Once she owned a very special "sculpture" by
Marcel Broodthaers: a square brick chimney, about
three feet high and one and one-half feet wide, with a
trowel stuck into the side of it. She hated to sell it, and
I wanted so to buy it at her cost of $15,000. But where
could it go? On another occasion, for the same price,
she had an Oldenburg "Toothbrush" maquette, perhaps seven feet high. In each of these cases, I'd probably
have found a rationale for exceeding my flexible monetary guidelines, but I lacked a plausible site. Today
each of those pieces are priceless, which was easily pre-
dictable. That was never a consideration to me.

Marian used to uncover unique objects: One time she had part of an edition of tables made by Meret Oppenheim (famed for her Fur-lined Teacup). Each is entirely gilded in gold, oval in shape (66" × 53"), with a dozen large bird-claw tracks embedded in the top surface and supported by two spindly avian legs, at the end of which are splayed talons. I would never consider parting with my table!

Since Marian was so considerate with me, I'd try to reciprocate. One year, in the '70s, art sales were sluggish and Marian had a problem: Sol LeWitt, who had recently married and moved to Spoleto, Italy, had need of ready cash. Marian and I both liked and admired him so much that we wanted to be of service, so I ended up buying over 200 prints and photos from many separate editions published over the years, none of which I had bought previously. (I already had several dozen.) Thereby, Sol ended up with $15,000 and I had a trove of unwanted great multiples and photographs. When all the boxes arrived in Cincinnati, I sent them right on to the CAM for display and/or storage—and these eventually became part of my larger gift. Sadly, the museum showed almost none of them. When the museum requested an auction appraisal of LeWitt's work from Christie's, the auction listed them as having NSV—no special value!

Marian had an annual Valentine's Day special exhibit and once I made some suggestions she liked very much. I remember selecting some enchanting watercolors (at Betty Parsons Gallery) by Richard Tuttle, whose work was normally priced out of my reach. They were deft, small abstractions, on lightly lined notepad paper, framed in crude, raw wood lath. Another choice was the photography of Susan Eder, a talented lady whose whimsical items I had first seen in a gallery at Wellfleet, Cape Cod. To help ensure success, both Marian and I bought examples of each artist's work (Tuttle's *Valentine II*, 1983; 26.6 × 15 cm; Eder's *Origami Beef Butchering*; collage of 12 chromogenic development [Ektachrome] prints, 18.3 × 35.4 cm; and *Origami Frog Dissection*; collage of 16 chromogenic development [Ektachrome] prints, 35.4 × 24.6 cm).

Marian gave Susan Eder a one-person show the following summer in her print room, and once again I couldn't resist and bought more photos. A favorite was *A Year at a Glance* (1981; 69.5 × 79.7 cm). She had shot the same segment of sky each day at the same hour, for an entire year, so the large collage represented a "weather map" that revealed eloquently the seasonal changes.

One day Marian telephoned me in Cincinnati and asked if I would be willing to sell Jennifer Bartlett's *Graceland Mansions*. To my surprise, the Getty Museum wanted it, which seemed a very unusual request from such an august institution. Seemingly, I had the only available one of a small edition, since the others were owned by other museums.

I knew the "Getty" had deep pockets and would pay handsomely for what they sought, so I was sorely tempted. Besides, it remained the favorite of my office personnel, which distressed me; I had tired of it long ago.

Haughtily I replied that I had an inflexible rule *never* to sell art (violated several times a few years later), but that I would be willing to swap the Getty for a Gerhard Richter "candle painting." I had watched his career over the years and greatly respected his talent, which was vastly underrated by the art world. He painted in many different styles—photo-realist, abstract, color-field—all of the highest quality. While relatively inexpensive, his prices were always slightly higher than I was willing to pay. In fact, I once almost bought a "candle" along with Anne Rorimer for the Chicago Art Institute, but his then-dealer, Angela Westwater, wouldn't budge. Anne got hers and Richter's price kept rising after my failure. So I had it firmly in mind to acquire one someday.

Marian scoured the world for some months and finally found two candle paintings in Europe—she bought one for herself and conveyed the other to me on behalf of the Getty (*Single Candle*, 1982; oil on canvas; 65.4 × 82 cm). As I gazed at it admiringly on my wall, the flickering flame of a single taper would mesmerize me. The painting was a real jewel.

At the end of the decade, dealer Jack Tilton visited me and spotted the Richter; he told me that "candle paintings" commanded enormous sums and it would be a great time for me to dispose of it. I told him I wouldn't consider it, but when he mentioned $150,000, I began to waver. Persuasively, he mentioned that my "candle" was really not THAT unique, since Richter had painted about forty canvases, depicting one, two or three candles on each. That argument finally convinced me, since the staggering sum would fatten my scholarship fund and help to educate many minority students. In a happy denouement, Jack made the sale and made a tidy profit for himself. The late '80s were incredible times.

John Weber

While John Weber and I never became personal friends, we had many coincidences in our lives. We both had married Romans—he with the art dealer Annina Nosei, I with Nori Castaldi. On comparing notes, we agreed that we had temperamental spouses. We each had summer homes on the Argentario along the Tuscan shore—he in Ansidonia and I at adjacent Porto Ercole.

John Weber had the sharpest eye for young talent in the business. Tibor de Nagy, Sidney Janis and Leo Castelli have all proved their mettle in the past, but John continues year in and year out to discover and sponsor unknown artists. Either in the "Project Room" or main gallery, a discerning, adventurous collector will be richly rewarded by the offerings, which range from American contemporary to Australian aborigines art.

Not only did I acquire the mainstays—such as Sol LeWitt—but many far more obscure: In 1978, I received an excited phone call from Cora Rosevear, who was attending the opening of a young artist, Alice Aycock, at the Weber Gallery. It was the only time she ever recommended a purchase. "Bob, you have to get a set of five magnificent drawings by this incredible artist!" So I bought *The Queen's Complex*, 1978, from *I Have Tried to Imagine the Kind of City You and I Could Live In as King and Queen*. (The central panel measured 107.3 × 182.9 cm. Two flanked each side, 91.3 × 60.9 cm apiece.) I believe that only the large structure was ever constructed, although Alice had high hopes that she might see her whole dream executed. She and I became rather close friends, and a long time later I commissioned a major site-specific work for my garden.

John introduced me to the sculpture of James Biederman and I acquired a wall structure from his debut show (*Untitled*, August 1979; oil, gesso and wood; 142.2 × 17.8 × 14.5 cm).

Another time John Weber (with Barbara Toll Gallery) introduced me to Stephen Campbell, a young Scotsman. His uniformly large paintings were brilliantly executed and I became very excited to own one by such an obvious budding star (*After The Hunt*, 1982; oil on canvas; 274.22 × 304.8 cm). It portrayed two sturdy men atop a barren hillock, with a dead stag at their feet. One figure is in hunting garb, the other in mod city clothes, with his arm inexplicably in a sling. A haunting, enigmatic image.

Campbell enjoyed instant success and received well-deserved homage from a fickle art world. His dual shows sold out quickly and his prices immediately doubled, trebled, and even quadrupled. I didn't keep track of his progress, but always assumed that he would reach new heights. Recently as I thumbed through auction catalogues, I've seen several wonderful paintings of Stephen Campbell up for sale. The "auction estimate" in each case was approximately what I had originally paid. It serves as a classic example of how cruelly and illogically the "art market" can punish a great artist.

John Weber's eclectic taste afforded collectors rich dividends. He represented a fine Italian painter, Lucio Pozzi, who one year spent a holiday in the Caribbean. On his return, Pozzi showed his dealer a series of watercolors he had made during his leisure hours. He had no intention of having them shown, since they were totally atypical of his usual style, but John found them so entrancing that he insisted on displaying them in a mini-exhibit. John was so right, and I bought two of them, each entitled *Negril Jamaica*, 1977 (36 × 47.9 cm).

Leo Castelli

My contact with Castelli Gallery has been so tenuous that only Leo Castelli's lofty stature in the art world warrants his inclusion. I doubt that he would recognize my name or face, despite countless meetings. Each time he acknowledges our introduction with Old World courtesy, as befits one stranger to another. Although I speak Italian rather fluently, he obviously prefers English; I have often wondered if he is perhaps *anti*-Italian, since I can't recall his showing anything by a compatriot.

The gallery space is forbidding, although one bright, friendly face occasionally appears: The gallery director, Susan Brundage, is the soul of affability and devoid of pretension. Frequently she has chided me about my attitude toward the gallery and the fact that I employ other dealers to buy in my behalf, a practice I indulged in flagrantly to make an obvious point to them about my cavalier treatment.

One day Paula Cooper and I were extolling the ability of Richard Artschwager, whom we saw as being vastly unappreciated. He had a show on at Castelli's, so we walked down the street to pay a visit. Paula bought

82

a splendid "gray" painting of a desolate railroad track for herself, and for me she got a wall structure that I thought to be quite special (*Untitled (Window)*, 1966; formica and wood; 61 × 91.4 × 12.7 cm). As my "buying agent" completed the transactions, the atmosphere was definitely chilly; but I was happy she made a nice profit, without any cost to me.

This approach was repeated several times with a bit more subtlety; I can recall only one occasion when I bought something from Brundage, who personally deserved better of me: It was a work on paper by Robert Barry, which I think was mispriced since it cost only a few hundred dollars (*Untitled*, 1979; pen and white ink on red paper; 45.7 × 45.5 cm).

One day in 1989 I strolled through the galleries of the "420" building, viewing a variety of exhibits. Castelli was showing the work of Ed Ruscha, whose slick airbrush puns had never captured my fancy. I barely glanced at the paintings, as I had struck up a conversation with Susan Brundage, who happened to be on the gallery floor, when she called my attention to one in particular. About 48″ × 60″, it had a succinct message: painted in two large letters was "J.R." Since my name happens to be J. R. Orton, Jr.—thereby boasting

83

TWO JRs—fate had seemed to indicate that I should possess it!

Susan informed me that the coveted treasure had been reserved for Leo Castelli, who dearly wanted it, but if I wished to purchase it, she would try to prevail on her boss to relinquish it. With a prod from her, I assented and a few minutes later, I learned that Signor Castelli had bowed out graciously and that I was the proud owner of *J.R.* for the paltry sum of $7,000.

I returned to California in a state of remorse at what I had done so impetuously; no sooner had I arrived home than I started seeing the Ruscha name touted in newspapers and art periodicals. The Castelli show had rave notices and suddenly an artist who had languished for years became red-hot. I waited for months for the arrival of *J.R.* and, when it wasn't forthcoming, I assumed that it had been sold elsewhere to a more favored client.

Six months later, I found myself in the elevator with Leo Castelli as we both headed for his gallery. I made some caustic remark about never having received my masterpiece, which surprised him greatly. A quick investigation revealed that it had been sitting all that time in a storeroom due to some snafu. My uncharitable thoughts were groundless and inexcusable.

When it finally arrived in La Jolla, the giant *J.R.* overwhelmed the rooms of my house. Wherever we tried placing it, the result was dreadful. I had bought a real lemon. So we temporarily leaned the painting against the entryway wall, where it blocked passage, and pondered how to get rid of the odious object.

Two days later I received a visit from a friend and former student, Henry Vincent, who had recently moved to L.A. Hank is a fine artist, now quite successful, but at the time he moonlighted at some of the galleries and tried to pick up some money trading art. Ever alert, he spotted my rejection. (Actually, it was hard to miss.)

Hank: "Bob, you have a *RUSCHA*. He's the hottest artist in California and there are none around. I can sell it in a minute."

Me (cool): "I just bought that from Castelli and it has just arrived. How can you expect me to let go of it?"

Hank: "Please! I can get you $12,000 and make something for myself. Be a friend."

Me: "Well, since you put it that way, I'll probably do it, but I want a day or so to think it over."

Actually, while secretly elated, I had developed gnawing guilt feelings about having taken *J.R.* away from Castelli. So I called Susan in New York and told her I didn't want the painting and could resell it; but perhaps she'd like me to return it to the gallery. An hour later she instructed me to sell it, as Castelli had chosen another Ruscha painting instead.

Usually, in my business, when I made bad purchases the market punished me mercilessly—and here I was miraculously showing a respectable profit. Hank sold *J.R.* to the Corcoran Gallery and received a modest commission. Soon afterwards the gallery sold it for $60,000.

The "Ruscha" phenomenon exemplifies rather well what transpired in those heady boom times, when art became a commodity for speculation. His prices followed a statistician's classic "bell-shaped curve," ending back where they originally started.

Sperone Westwater Gallery

Angela Westwater, a source of many of my purchases, is a shining example of how an intelligent dealer can be of service to a collector. She always kept in mind what

I might want and came up with an item I sought at an appropriate cost. Thanks to her, I acquired a fine wall sculpture by Donald Judd (*Untitled*, 1974; anodized green aluminum; 12.7 × 101.6 × 21.6 cm). In that case, she found it available for quick resale and I found a pretext to fly to New York and personally inspect it. Only by her quick response could I acquire a seminal work that would have normally been far beyond my means. (I gave the sculpture to the CAM in 1985. I just bought a similar work, reasonably priced, at Christie's last fall, which adorns the outer wall of my house's covered loggia and looks stunning.) Seemingly Judd is another artist who "doesn't do well at auction," despite a towering reputation.

Another time, through the joint kindness of Angela and Marian Goodman, I acquired a strong abstract painting by Gerhard Richter, full of swirling brush strokes in primary colors (*Untitled*, 1984; oil on canvas; 65.4 × 80 cm). I showed the good sense to hold onto it and it now graces a wall of my sitting room.

When I negotiated with Michael Singer to create a major work on my La Jolla hillside, Angela (who represents him) stepped aside graciously and permitted us to deal directly together without any benefit to her. So I have lots of reasons to compliment her for a generous nature and high professional conduct.

Max Protetch

I got to know Max Protetch very well, particularly since I served as his consultant in the days when he was undercapitalized and skated on thin ice. Of all the dealers I have known, he has come closest to thinking like a businessman, treating art as a means of gaining profit. He has a good sense of the value of real estate, which led him to favorable purchases and rental agreements with exquisite timing. Max's good sense and prudence have enabled him to build capital methodically, allowing him to weather the current economic storm without major discomfort.

He has a deep appreciation for art and has nurtured the artists in his stable with caring and persistence, which has paid liberal dividends for everyone involved. He represents many people whom I respect greatly. Two of my favorites have been Siah Armajani and Scott Burton, who were close friends and collaborated on a massive project at Battery Park. I bought a lot of Scott's work elsewhere, but Max sold me a great wall-piece of Siah's (*Notations For Reading Garden #1*, 1980–81; balsa and paint on Astro-Turf and cardboard; 93.1 × 139 cm).

Max always struck me as rather diffident by nature, but he demonstrated how wrong I could be. Several years ago, Scott Burton contracted AIDS, which led him to a lingering, excruciating death. During that dreadful period, Max showed our dear mutual friend a solicitousness and tenderness that astounded me. During the final months, he visited the hospital each day to bolster Scott's sinking morale. In fact, Scott refused to let anyone else see him in such a degraded condition; try as I might, my proffer of a visit was summarily rejected, although we had been close for a long time.

Another friend of Max's was Nick Wilder, once a prominent West Coast dealer, who also became ill. He became a painter in his waning years and Max loyally displayed his work, which was more than competent. Too, Max doggedly promoted the paintings of David Reed over many years and the persistence paid off, as Reed eventually received the recognition he deserved.

The Max Protetch Gallery has specialized in selling the working drawings of prominent architects. An early coup for Max was obtaining contents of the estate of

Frank Lloyd Wright, and Max did an outstanding marketing job that brought millions of dollars into the Wright Foundation, as well as singular benefits to himself. Japanese buyers poured fortunes into his coffers as the result of an exhibition in Tokyo.

To my mind, most architects are really frustrated artists, without the talent to depict a salable object. For that reason, the main clients for architectural drawings are fellow architects. No one else in their right minds would pay lofty prices for such boring, unintelligible tripe. (I can't make head or tail out of schemata depicting stairwells, upstairs and downstairs rooms, etc.) I lump all of the big shots into the same category, be it Venturi, Gehry or Graves. My dim view of the exceedingly profitable niche that Max had developed caused endless squabbles between us, as he defined the sublime characteristics I failed to appreciate.

However, I found one notable exception—an architect who could draw like a whiz. Aldo Rossi, winner of the Pritzker Award as "architect of the year" in 1990, is one of the most noted practitioners in Europe: He could well have been in the wrong profession, he is so multitalented. I had to use self-control to buy only two drawings, each of which depicted aspects of specific projects: *Sagu Palm*, 1976 (22.6" × 32.4"), and *The Lighthouse*, 1980, from *Monuments of Venice*, 1981. *The Lighthouse* is derived from a large undertaking on the Lido and represents fanciful tall cabanas, with colorful pennants flying.

Max has a seductive way of tempting me: One day he set up a carousel of slides, all representing the work of Mary Miss, dating from the '60s. The sculptures had been in storage for a long time and he felt remiss in not having sold them. Most had been documented in publications and each was better than the last. I ended up selecting just one, an abstracted "ladder" with two poles, wider at the bottom, narrower at the top, held together by a wide, inwardly curved steel plate. As it must rest against a wall, and RSM had no space, it went immediately to the CAM (*Untitled*, 1967; wood and steel; 304.8 × 91.4 cm).

Too often, Max would talk me into buying something I could not install at home or in the office. Just last year he started representing my good friend Andrew Spence, who left Barbara Toll Gallery after a painful separation. Andy produces meticulous, minimal paintings, which he works and reworks in a snail slow gestation period. He had just finished his largest work ever

91

and it was quite special—in fact, so special that the Metropolitan Museum wanted it. So his dealer deduced that I would be a likely candidate to act as donor; actually, it didn't take a lot of persuasion, because I couldn't think of a more worthy person I'd want to help (*China*, 1992; diptych; 108″ × 36″).

My all-time favorite "Max" story involved the artist Jackie Ferrara. One day he called me with a very sad tale: From experience he knew that whenever Exxon bought an important work of art for its collection, Mobil would mirror the purchase by acquiring a similar item by the same artist. Therefore, when Max learned that Exxon was committed to buying a huge wooden structure from La Ferrara, he instructed her to make a second one of roughly equal size—though of different configuration, of course.

The Exxon sale went through smoothly, but to Max's despair Mobil had instituted a serious retrenchment due to flagging earnings, and forewent the honor of buying the sculpture targeted at them. He had to do something rather quickly since he had to remove the unsold object from his gallery, and putting the giant in storage would entail hideous, ongoing expenses. This monster was titled *Pi-Red*, 1979, made of fir lumber, and measuring a tidy 358.1 × 210.8 × 210.8 cm. (In fact, a child could easily crawl through an aperture at the bottom of the towering sculpture.)

Patiently hearing out Max's litany of woe, I asked him sweetly how his dilemma could possibly be of more than cursory interest to me, who would offer only friendly sympathy.

Max answered brightly: "But of course YOU are going to buy it."

Me, tartly: "Max, you're out of your mind, I wouldn't know what to do with it—and besides, the cost would be prohibitive. You know that."

Max, soothingly: "I have it all worked out. The Cincinnati Art Museum would love to have the piece and it's at a price you can't resist."

Me, annoyed: "How on earth would you know that the CAM wants it? I've never spoken to them about it; in fact, I didn't know the sculpture existed until just now."

That unprincipled rascal had gone behind my back to negotiate a gift without saying a word to me. Although it violated just about every ethical principle I could bring to mind, I found it impossible to remain annoyed, since Max is ingenious and funny. Also, since I have been a salesman too, I rather admired his incredible moxie.

The conversation that ensued violated all my precepts about not bargaining over art. At least in *that* regard he had met his peer, since I've been a trader all my life. The price dropped precipitously, as I knew I had him over a barrel, until I finally arrived at $10,000— far more than I had ever paid for anything. After consultation with the poor artist, who would be the principal one to suffer, Max called me back and said: "The piece is on a truck, headed for Cincinnati." I wouldn't have been surprised if it had been loaded the day *before*, since he was in such a desperate spot.

The CAM *did* love the Ferrara sculpture and installed it in a large, high-domed gallery in a place of honor. But their enthusiasm must have waned, for ten years later they foolishly sent the sculpture to Christie's for auction with a pathetic "reserve" price. Since it would not fit into many living rooms, not unsurprisingly there were no bids whatsoever. Now, more than three years later, it probably sits in Christie's warehouse. If the CAM had offered the piece to Michael Klein, Ferrara's current dealer, he might well have placed the sculpture in some museum. It is an excellent sculpture, but there would be few appropriate repositories for that large a work.

Sonnabend Gallery

I always found a cordial reception at Sonnabend, although I never developed even a minimal personal rapport with the owners. Ileana Sonnabend always nodded cordially in recognition and, if we shook hands, the social courtesy reminded me of a Japanese who was more accustomed to bowing. However, Antonio Homem is always the soul of affability and more than helpful. He always waxed eloquent indiscriminately about the gallery artists, althouth their works range from the sublime to the execrable.

I'm sure that I am not the first to question how Sonnabend decides which artist to show. Considering the refinement of taste so obviously demonstrated, I come to the conclusion that financial considerations are of considerable importance.

To name just a few of their stars, I think of Jannis Kounellis, Mel Bochner—as well as Anne and Patrick Poirier and Robert Morris. Three great conceptual

95

photographers are represented as well: John Baldessari, the Bechers, and Gilbert and George. At the other end of the spectrum, in the abyss of the art world, stand Jeff Koons, Ashley Bickerton, Chaim Vaisman and Terry Winters.

Jeff Koons stands alone for his tawdry, prurient bad taste, and reams have been written on the subject that certainly draws notoriety to the gallery. The other three —Bickerton, Vaisman and Winters—may draw howls of protest from their loyal buyers, but I stick to my opinion: undistinguished and trite.

Despite my feelings, I feel gratitude for the wonderful objects I bought at the gallery, and the patient guidance from which I benefited over many years. How I wish Sonnabend would adopt a "Just Say No!" policy.

The photographic works of Hilla and Bernd Becher are so wonderful that I established the custom of buying one group each year. The two were obsessed by common structures such as water towers, mine pitheads, grain elevators or European stucco houses, with wooden beams crisscrossing their sides. Each series would be mounted in a set of six, nine, or an even larger number. The size of the prints varied as well.

The Bechers typified the obsessive, compulsive nature of so many artists. They traversed Europe and the States far and wide with their young son in tow, living in a commodious van while they sought out new subjects to shoot. Being perfectionists, they would wait at a site for an absolutely cloudless sky and then take a photograph that was always perfectly centered! I don't believe they ever retouched or cropped a print. They must have slaved over many options to come up with a beautifully balanced set of prints.

Cora Rosevear once invited Hilla Becher and me to lunch at the MOMA dining room, since she knew how much I respected their artistry. I found a modest, charming lady, eminently likable. To my surprise, she knew of my numerous purchases and complimented me on my choices. She felt that I had picked her favorites each year, and that I had the best selection extant. I had to confess that it happened by accident: I had never attended one of the Sonnabend shows, but at their closing Antonio would send me transparencies of what remained unsold and from these leftovers I made my decision. This led to a general discussion as to how an artist's best work often remains unsold, a phenomenon I have seen operating too often to be labeled a coincidence.

At that time the Bechers couldn't make a decent wage from their art and they both taught school—Bernd at a German university, which caused painful family separations—but their expenses were modest and somehow they mucked along, dedicated to their mission. This shocked me, because they were already well known and several prestigious books had documented their work, but prices were low and sales slow.

I learned from Hilla that she and her husband contemplated a trip to the Midwest to photograph water towers and coal mine pitheads in Kentucky, so I insisted that they stay with me and use our house as a base of operations. They showed up with their son at my home in Cincinnati and with incredible, self-effacing modesty declined to use the proffered bedrooms, saying they would be quite comfortable in their van. So for several weeks they parked in the spacious driveway between excursions into the hinterland.

It affords me great pleasure to report that today the Bechers have reached lofty status in the art world and their photographs command the high prices they always deserved, so I think that they have finally achieved financial security with plenty to spare. It couldn't have happened to two nicer people.

Edward Thorp

Edward Thorp is a tall man—perhaps 6′3″—of pleasant mien and a quite affable, ingratiating manner. I first met him at his small gallery on West Broadway when I purchased a painting by Eric Fischl. Shortly afterwards he obtained a huge space above the U.S. post office on Prince Street at very favorable terms, renting for a long period of time.

He became a client of mine; as his consultant I spent many hours with him planning how best to utilize so many square feet. At the time, he had an impressive list of loyal, satisfied customers who bought regularly at his suggestion. Eric Fischl's explosion upon the art scene gave Ed an enormous boost, and David True, a fine painter, had a growing reputation, with steadily increasing prices.

April Gornik, Fischl's companion, had a blossoming career and her first show was a sell-out, except for one large painting that no one seemed to want because of its size. I acquired it, and it stands out as one of the greatest canvases I ever bought—and possibly the best she ever produced. It depicts a vast storm in the distance, with solid gray clouds sweeping across the top

99

edge and five downspouts, of the same menacing color, touching the floor of the desert. The space between glows with an eerie reflection of the sun, and straight across the foreground is a deep rust desert floor interspersed with low tufts of sagebrush (*Storm Crossing the Desert*, 1983; oil on canvas; 152.3 × 365.8 cm). It is truly an epic work!

Early in my relationship with Ed, it became quite obvious that our artistic sensibilities were poles apart. While Ed showed fine work, I felt none of it suitable for the offices of RSM; yet, in a brief period of time I bought a number of works from the Thorp Gallery. I had a rule never to buy anything I really disliked, but I was willing to acquire a work that might be considered important for a museum collection, even if it were something I wouldn't consider owning personally.

Invariably, I would pay an amount that went directly to the artist, and Ed Thorp made no profit at all. Everything would be shipped directly to the CAM and, in most cases, the size of the painting precluded RSM showing it if that were my wish (it wasn't). He always came up with persuasive reasons why I should help him or the artist and, since I had grown very fond of him, I bent over backwards to oblige. Since I bought at

100

roughly half the retail price, I could make a gift and come out relatively unscathed—and, if prices rose, I'd do a bit better after holding the work a few years.

In the case of April Gornik, Ed wanted eagerly to have a sell-out and was delighted that I bought the painting at his cost. A ten-footer wouldn't be easy to sell. April probably never knew what transpired between me and her dealer. This transaction set a pattern for the future.

Ed could have several shows simultaneously, since the space was so enormous and he often had group shows of people he respected or of friends he wished to help. Over time he offered a rich palette of choices to collectors, who seemed to enjoy patronizing his gallery. Much of this dizzying array ended up in my lap.

Ed showed the large paintings of Anton Van Dalen, for many years assistant to Saul Steinberg. They were really wonderful, but I had no earthly use for them. One portrayed an automobile driving through a hole in a giant redwood tree. Another was even more appealing: A proud chicken strutting in the foreground of a white-tiled kitchen. Nothing sold and Ed beseeched me to buy one. So I bought the massive chicken (*Silver Wyandotte Chicken*, 1984; oil on canvas; 121.9 × 162.9 cm).

Later I gave the CAM that chicken—which I always regretted, though I don't know what I'd have done with it. They sold it at "auction" for something like $30. I tried fruitlessly to retrieve it.

One day Thorp came to me with a tragic tale: He had sold a painting of his friend Gary Bower to a couple in Connecticut—which permitted the artist to afford taking his family to Europe for the summer. When the picture arrived, however, the buyers recanted because it was too large for their living room. (It WAS indeed large.) Now Bower faced paying for the air tickets, and his travel plans were totally disrupted, so could I please help out?

Bower, who taught at Oberlin College, had a fine reputation and I knew him by name. Certainly he didn't deserve such a fate. The specific painting had been shown at the Cleveland Contemporary Art Museum and was featured in their catalogue of his one-person show. It looked just great to me, so of course I bought it. When I finally saw the painting, it was as good as I had hoped (*Theories of War: Focus 1980*; oil and acrylic on canvas; 233.4×293 cm).

This too was later deaccessioned and sold at "auction" by the CAM. I believe it brought $40, reputedly bought by one of the auction house staff, who claimed to have cut it up for use of the canvas, as she was an amateur "Sunday painter."

Another artist I helped was Joseph Santore, a serious, competent painter whose work was shown by Ed Thorp. I got to know him and his wife—both of them fine people—when they made a trip to California. His show with Ed didn't do all that well, so once again I helped a worthy artist by buying his painting (*Bouillabaisse*, 1983–84; oil on canvas; 81.7×99.2 cm). A finely worked still-life, it was not to my taste, but definitely a good painting.

On one occasion, to reciprocate for my assistance, Ed did me a great favor: He found a superb painting for me by John McLaughlin (at a low price), which I adored having.

Ed seems to have a fatal flaw that I have not been able to identify: For some reason his best, most lucrative artists have always left him for other galleries. Certainly Eric Fischl departed with blandishments from Mary Boone that entailed magabucks. David True is more puzzling, because he and Ed were intimate friends and they had done well together. True departed for

Blum Helman. The latter gallery developed Brian Hunt and Donald Sultan but more recently is noted for enticing established artists to their gallery rather than developing talent on their own.

One day, after various setbacks, Ed's spirits soared when he received a phone call from David Deutsch, a childhood friend from school days. Deutsch had been showing with Annina Nosei and his career had been proceeding apace; however, since he and Annina had a stormy clash of temperaments, he decided to make a change.

According to Ed, Deutsch came from a wealthy family and had no shortage of funds, but he felt that Annina priced his work too low, considering his burgeoning recognition. So they agreed upon a quantum leap for his first show at Edward Thorp Gallery, with prices ranging $10,000–12,000 for rather large canvases— or roughly double what he had been obtaining recently. Their accord was reached in early winter and a show of six paintings was scheduled for May.

In early April I received a telephone call from Ed, who was in Paris. In great distress, he needed advice, having just had a devastating conversation with David Deutsch. Deutsch had been convinced by Joe Helman that his talent was vastly underrated and that the prices of his next show were ridiculously low. If David joined HIS gallery, Helman told him, the paintings would be sold for $25,000–35,000. (This was well before the boom that followed later.) So Deutsch had decided to make an immediate change before the opening of his May show. I advised Ed to flatly reject the proposal immediately and, since the announcements of the upcoming exhibit had been mailed, "the show would go on" as planned, at the prices already established. After that Deutsch would be free to do as he pleased, since there was no written or oral contract to the contrary.

The other parties had no alternative but to accept Thorp's terms, particularly since the six paintings were already in his possession, but he faced immediate pressure to turn over unsold paintings after the show to Blum Helman. In response to that demand, I devised a delicious ploy, potentially quite beneficial to him.

Since, quite frequently, sales do not occur until after an exhibit has closed, I wanted Ed to gain precious time, so I instructed him to inform David Deutsch at the closing date that all the paintings had been sold. Meanwhile, I would allow Ed Thorp six months in which to sell all the paintings and, if any were unsold by that time, I'd take them at his cost and send them to the CAM. At that time he could settle his account with Deutsch.

This gave Ed a great window of opportunity, since in the interim the art world would know of the new alliance and resultant increased pricing of David Deutsch's work. If somehow Ed didn't sell any of them, I would have an outstanding bargain and, on that rare occasion, make a handsome profit when I made my gift.

Ed loved the opportunity I afforded him, but even with the incredible sales pitch available, by autumn only four paintings had been sold. I thought they would have sold rather quickly, but I ended up with two big paintings that, as usual, were shipped directly to the CAM. I found both landscapes rather insipid; they were certainly not anything I'd normally dream of buying, but the recipient appeared to appreciate them (*Gerry Park*, 1982; oil on paper mounted on canvas; 36″ × 120″; and *Estate*, 1984; water-based paint on paper mounted on linen; 81″ × 127¾″).

Ed Thorp returned from a trip to Europe, where he had uncovered a rare opportunity offered by a German dealer: he could buy a considerable quantity of work by two elderly Frenchmen, the philosopher/painter Henri Michaux—certainly not unknown—and Eugène Leroy. Henri Michaux produced rather ethereal abstract froms and Leroy applied thick layers of paint, probably with a knife, to produce rather dingy, dark-hued works in which one could faintly recognize the human form. Neither sent my heart pulsating, but Ed saw a chance to do very well so, not being a dealer nor knowing what sells, who was I to argue.

I don't recall precisely the amount involved, but Ed had to come up with about $60,000 right away—which he didn't have, so I volunteered to finance the transaction, for which I would receive 12 percent interest per annum on what he owed me, plus a modest share of the profit, if any.

The venture was ill-fated from the beginning, and Ed's optimism faded as neither artist's work sold well. The time clock kept ticking inexorably, as the interest due me mounted and I had received no repayment of capital. At one point I agreed to take a small portrait by Leroy and reduce the amount he owed me by $5,000—but, on thinking it over, I changed my mind as I didn't really like it at all. While a change of heart is not uncommon among collectors, Thorp took umbrage at my decision and constantly held it up to me—possibly to get me on the defensive.

Our relationship deteriorated badly, as so often happens between friends in money matters. He threw up to me all the rare "steals" I had made, totally forgetting how my purchases had come about, yet he certainly had a point regarding the Fischl painting *Grief*, which had become quite valuable (though paltry, compared to what it would have been appraised for if I had waited a few years before donating it to the CAM).

I pressed Ed hard to liquidate an inventory of salable paintings I knew he owned and thereby reimburse me the amount he owed. Slowly, but surely, over time he paid me off, but at the end there was the matter of unpaid interest, amounting to over $20,000. (If I calculated properly the interest on unpaid interest, it would have been substantially more.)

After increasingly acrimonious, heated arguments, I visited Ed to settle the matter conclusively. He told me that he had consulted with his laywer, who advised him that he owed me nothing, after taking into consideration the profits I had earned through him (negligible).

I replied: "Ed, I think I've always acted as your

friend. Let's leave your lawyer out of this. Do YOU feel you have an obligation to me? If the answer is affirmative, I'll give you plenty of time to pay me back."

Ed: "I feel I owe you nothing, but as a show of goodwill, I'll give you this Leroy painting (he pointed to a small work leaning against the wall). It is worth $5,000 and if you hold it a few years, it'll easily be worth $20,000 or more."

After that rejoinder, I rose from my chair and walked out of the room without the painting. At my stage in life, I didn't need a condescending sop from one Edward Thorp. This transpired in 1989 and I've never seen him again.

Diane Brown

I first met Diane Brown—a single mother with two small children in tow—when she moved from Washington to New York. It was a courageous act on her part, but she was determined to open a gallery specializing in sculpture, and the time was ripe, based on her experience in D.C. She obtained a modest space, just opposite our Greene Street loft and, finding her ambitious, agreeable and perennially cheerful, I tried to be of assistance. For a brief spell, I acted as her consultant, but her chief problem was that she needed live bodies to buy from her, and that I couldn't solve.

Yet over time I think I was useful: I introduced her to Joel Fisher, with whom she was personally intimate for a spell, and he became a mainstay of the gallery until the bitter end. Also, I helped her with Jan Groth, whose drawings and sculptures sold well. (Previously I had put Jan together with Marian Goodman and she had given him a show just at the time he was featured at the Guggenheim Museum. Strangely, even then his work didn't attract buyers.)

In good times, Brown flourished and moved to possible the best-designed quarters in New York, on the second floor of 560 Broadway. We became closer personally and several times she and her kids came to La Jolla to visit—and we dined together occasionally at her New York loft. I never was really a patron, principally since I dealt directly with Joel Fisher, which she accepted cheerfully, for she knew our friendship far preceded her.

What happened to Diane Brown during the sickening downward spiral of the art market might serve as a microcosm of what has occurred in many cities lately. When she closed forever in 1991 (she had by that time another roomy space in Tribeca), she left behind a couple of walking-wounded, for whom I feel partially responsible. While I have no reason to question her intentions, I am left with the feeling that she acted irresponsibly in several instances.

One day I paid a call on Diane's last gallery and she moaned about the dearth of business. She and other dealers were operating in a total vacuum, without signs of a turnaround. She had some interesting work by Lauren Ewing that had cost a fortune to construct. Would I please buy one and at least help the artist partially recover her expenses? Ewing had constructed several faux-Chippendale pieces of furniture. The best was an oversized secretary, meticulously crafted, in the back of which was an electronic bullhorn that could be used to spew messages through a speaker concealed within.

It was the first time I had heard of the artist, but I telephoned Hugh Davies, director of the La Jolla Museum, to ask if he would be interested in having the piece in his collection. He recognized the work immediately and responded enthusiastically, saying he felt positive that the acquisitions committee would readily approve the promised gift. So I obliged Diane, and once again purchased a monumental "sculpture."

Time passed and I heard that Diane had closed the

gallery. Not much later, I had a visit in California from a New York artist who was a friend of Lauren Ewing. Not knowing of my involvement with Diane, she proceeded to tell me how Diane had stiffed Lauren by not passing on a collector's cheque for a sale. It left me sick with frustration and anger.

More time elapsed, and one day I received a cheery phone call from Diane, soliciting me in behalf of some pet charity. I replied coldly that I wanted no further contact after what she had done to Lauren Ewing. Diane's excuse seemed rather lame: "When the cheque arrived, I deposited it in my account before paying the artist. Just at that moment the IRS froze my bank account because of a tax delinquency so I *couldn't* pay her. As soon as I can, I'll pay her every cent I owe." I answered: "When that day comes, feel free to call. Otherwise, please leave me alone." On May 13, 1992, Lauren Ewing did in fact receive a 40 percent partial payment from Diane Brown.

Diane Brown's gallery demise caused an even worse debacle, involving my dear friend George Lester.

George and I became intimate friends during World War II, when we joined the British army, trained in India and served in the Western Desert. After the war we both lived in Rome, he running his George Lester Gallery, I doing refugee work for UNRRA.

Later we both returned to the States, married, and each had two children. Our lives became deeply enmeshed in a widening family circle as we settled down; he got to know my family members and I became close to his brother, Charles, a diplomat, and his sister, Kitty, who lived in Florence with her painter husband, Renzo, and their attractive children.

George's beloved wife, Sophie, died suddenly when their children were young teens. In despair, he left their home in Old Lyme, Connecticut, and dropped totally out of sight. I heard vague rumors that he was trekking in Nepal or else wandering around the globe. We lost contact for years.

Much later, one Sunday morning I ran into George at Grand Central Station and he introduced me to his English bride, Anne, whom he had recently married. We three headed for Connecticut on the train and had a lively interaction as we brought each other up to date. Evidently, old emotional wounds had healed and the two lived contentedly in the countryside near New Haven.

113

Our conversation rambled over a wide range of topics, until he asked a rather abrupt question.

George: "Bobby, do you still have your keen interest in art?"

Me: "As a matter of fact, I do. I'm now collecting contemporary art."

George, musing: "I wonder what ever happened to that young fellow, Robert Smithson, whom I regarded so highly? By chance have you run across his name?"

Me, incredulous: "George, Smithson died quite young, but he is the hero of young artists interested in site-specific earthworks and a seminal figure who will be known through the ages!"

George, in his customary, low-keyed manner: "Well, that is interesting. I'm sure I have some of his work stored above the garage, so the next time you're in New York, come visit and we'll search around together while I'll tell you more about myself and Smithson." At that he and Anne disembarked at their station, after we exchanged telephone numbers.

I could scarcely contain my excitement before my excursion to Connecticut. Meanwhile, George had rummaged in the garage attic among a vast cache of art dating from his Roman period, and uncovered sixty oils and twelve paintings on paper, all by Robert Smithson. They were all neatly rolled up as they had been for possibly twenty years!

I had no pretensions about being an amateur art historian, but I had rather precise knowledge about Smithson's career, especially since I had done a bit of research in the interim. The bibliography of writings on Smithson extended for pages and pages.

What we viewed was a total shock: the outpouring of a deeply religious young man, who filled his paintings with biblical iconography. There were dragons chasing their tails, weird portraits of unidentifiable saints, swirling flames of fire and devilish figures. Without exception they were powerful, arresting works of a young genius, and totally atypical of his later efforts. Nothing we saw provided a minimal clue as to what Smithson later became.

When George and I returned to the house, over a drink he told me a fascinating tale. On a visit to New York in the late '40s, he had strolled up Madison Avenue with the vague intention of finding young artists whose work he might show at his gallery in Rome. On one stretch of the avenue there were quite a few dealers and he glanced in their windows for clues. Suddenly he became transfixed by a wonderful oil displayed, and entered the gallery to inquire about the artist. The owner told him that an engaging young man had brought the painting in, hoping for a buyer. Since the artist was obviously talented, on a whim the owner had stuck it in the window. He had the youngster's telephone number, but he knew absolutely nothing more about him.

So that was how George Lester met Robert Smithson, a vibrant, tortured lad, quite frustrated and ambitious. He visited the painter's decrepit studio and saw hosts of wonderful things, so George decided on the spot to pay Smithson a monthly stipend for living expenses and also to give him a one-person exhibit in Rome. Indeed, Smithson had a series of three annual shows, none of which proved a commercial success. My friend recalled only two sales he ever made, and the remainder of his work was what we had been examining.

When George concluded his discourse, he handed me a thick packet of letters, perhaps fifty or more, all from Robert Smithson, written over the term of their collaboration. Rifling through the contents, I saw a side to his persona that was totally concealed from public scrutiny. He was evidently a devout Roman Catholic, increasingly doubting of church tenets, and trying desperately to break loose from the bonds that tied him. Many missives revealed a terrible insecurity and a low self-confidence in his ability as an artist. His gratitude to George for moral and financial support seemed to be the deciding factor in keeping up his spirits. He referred constantly to his desire to come to Europe, perhaps for an opening—but, according to George, he never made the trip.

Without a doubt, the letters showed a Robert Smithson that was of historical importance, but in addition he had a compelling literary style that succinctly expressed philosophical thoughts and emotional responses.

When George moved back to the States in the '50s, he managed to completely lose contact with his protégé, whom he respected greatly, and of whom he had become very fond. So my news about Smithson's works had been the first he had heard in more than twenty years.

Inaccurately, I assessed the paintings to be worth a fortune, and correctly deemed the letters to have singular archival significance. Since George seemed rather lackadaisical about the thought of promoting the work, we struck an agreement: I would arrange to market Smithson's work with 25 percent of the proceeds

117

earmarked for our family foundation, "Earthward Bound," or for any alternative charity I designated.

My failure to ultimately publicize Robert Smithson's work is a lengthy story. The basic problem was that it de-mythicized an image he had built through later work and writings. His secular intellect was totally at variance with what had transpired earlier. His widow, the prominent artist Nancy Holt, dearly wished to maintain her husband as a cult figure, and bitterly opposed the publication of his letters or the showing of his early work. I learned that under modern copyright law, she could keep Smithson's correspondence with George out of the public domain, even though he was a third party with whom she was never involved or, in fact, even knew.

At one moment, Steingrim Laursen showed great enthusiasm for my project and could envision a grand tour of Smithson's paintings in Europe. He saw the oils personally and envisaged stunning sales that would benefit all parties; but when he faced stubborn opposition to the plan, he bowed out reluctantly.

Everyone I approached had the same attitude—until some years later when I brought up the subject with Diane Brown. Perhaps because she was not exactly in the mainstream of the art world, she showed no special compunction and was eager to exploit a huge potential. I introduced her to George and they made mutual arrangements to which I was not privy.

Enterprising and energetic, Diane had a Smithson show and arranged for quite a few works to tour Europe. According to George, she sold a few canvases for respectable sums, but I never knew the details and I stayed out of their mutual dealings at all times.

When I called Anne and George Lester in early 1994 to check on their well-being, Anne added a new and sordid chapter to the saga: At the time Diane closed her gallery she had an indeterminate amount of art stored at Crozier Fine Arts, a New York warehouse specializing in the field. Crozier had worked out a payment schedule with Diane, but apparently Crozier itself was in some financial difficulty. As a result, an insider at Crozier invested money into the organization and thus became the major decision maker there.

Unbeknownst to Diane Brown or the Lesters, but later uncovered by son Robert Lester, the new decision maker had brought in an expert from Sotheby's to evaluate Diane's holdings in the warehouse. The expert had put a high value on the Smithsons owned by the Lesters.

When the Lesters tried to retrieve some twenty-five paintings left on consignment with Diane and stored at

Crozier, the warehouse sent bill after escalating bill. The final fully escalated bill was over $60,000.

Tragically, George Lester's memory has faded and he is eerily disassociated from events. His son Robert was sufficiently incensed to take up the cudgel and defend his father's interests. He hired a lawyer and worked out a settlement with Crozier for less than one-tenth the escalated figure. When, however, Robert arrived to pick up the Smithsons, some of the paintings were missing. Without the Lesters' permission, a small selection of Smithsons had been taken to Sotheby's and were scheduled to be auctioned. At the last minute, with an attorney's help, the paintings were pulled from auction and given back to their rightful owners. Robert said that during this entire ordeal Diane Brown was extremely helpful. Still, my conscience bothers me that I caused intimate friends to suffer such a loss through my "good" offices.

Many other dealers deserve mention, although our relations may have been tenuous, but each contributed to my "learning curve"—usually in a positive way; on rare occasions, negatively. Some that come readily to mind are: Grace Borgenicht Gallery, Jack Tilton Gallery,

Graham Modern, Zabriske (long ago), Kurt Marcus, Joe Fawbush, Willard Gallery (closed), Xavier Fourcade (closed), Laurie Rubin (closed), and a host of others.

On the West Coast, there were B/C Space in Laguna Beach, TLK in Costa Mesa (closed), Mark Quint, Thomas Babeor and Soma Galleries in San Diego. In the Los Angeles area: Richard Kuhlenschmidt, Daniel Weinberg (mainly in San Francisco), Dorothy Goldeen, L.A. Louver, Asher/Faure, Rosamund Felsen and Margo Leavin.

In Chicago I had many pleasant engagements on various levels with Roberta Lieberman, of Zolle Lieberman Gallery.

It affords pleasure to think back on a variety of encounters I enjoyed over many years. Some outstanding dealers, like Margo Leavin, never made a specific sale to me, but we established a rapport and even a measure of mutual respect and friendship.

Peripheral Aspects of Collecting

When I become engrossed in a new passion, my attention span is not much better than a three-year-old's. Invariably the flame dies out and I'm off on another tangent. I had my "Japanese" period, my "Jugoslav" era, and a long spell devoted to public education and inner-city communities. Somehow I have sustained my interest in contemporary art longer than usual.

My all-consuming avidity to learn died out long ago. After all, I could only learn once what I didn't already know, so the thrill of discovery cannot be repeated. By an accident of fate, I immersed myself in the field at an ideal moment. There was an exciting burst of creativity, and prices were low enough not to deter a new collector.

Perhaps incorrectly, I diagnose the last decade as a rather barren time, with little of the spark and energy I confronted earlier. My opinion may be formulated by a sour, declining old man, but much of what is produced seems to lack a certain aesthetic quality I prize so highly. Political and social statements dominate the art scene, as young artists protest vehemently the indignities of our times.

Certainly an appropriate, even necessary, role for artists is to heighten our awareness of today's dominant issues such as sexism, racism, gay rights and AIDS, all of which the rich and bourgeois seem to callously ignore. Yet, when I find myself bombarded with strident

122

messages, their constant repetition tends to end up boring me. I have a strong prejudice against language being embodied in works of art, and if there are a plethora of words, I find my attention wandering as my eye moves on to something else. (I exclude masters of our language, such as Lawrence Weiner and John Baldessari.)

As a result, some of us old-timers dread attending the Whitney Biennial and other blockbusters such as Documenta in Kassel, Germany; it becomes quite depressing to view the oft-repeated themes, most of which are derivative from earlier polemicists. Hopefully I am not a fossilized dinosaur; I still feel the blood of an anarchist pulse through my veins and my outrage at injustice remains undiminished. Also, I like true originality —the more challenging, the better. Recent technological innovations permit marvelous manipulation of photographic images and video art—all quite exciting to me. But quite obviously much of what today passes as avant-garde leaves me cold.

To combat my ennui, I have devised a number of tactics that help sustain my flagging attention to contemporary art. Much of it stems from becoming involved on many levels and, at times, sponsoring off-beat projects. Perhaps a neophyte collector might glean some

123

useful tips that might widen horizons and enhance pleasure. An impetus for me was the principle that I should not just be a recipient of artworks, but devise ways in which I could give to the art world as well.

Maybe this has been the most rewarding part of a two-decade adventure, as new opportunities to contribute something constructive pop up with regularity. My part has been always on a modest scale, but as an admirer of E. F. Schumacher, I always think that "small is beautiful." Lately, my main thrust has been to help keep good artists afloat in parlous times, but in the past my assistance has taken various forms.

One of my most satisfying ventures was the "adoption" of Printed Matter, the unique and funky art book publisher and retail outlet on Lipsenard Street in Tribeca. Sol LeWitt left the place to me as a legacy when he moved to Italy, and Amy Baker, then publisher of *Art Forum*, twisted my arm as well. She headed the board and felt the institution was floundering just shy of an early demise.

The request came at a propitious time—in 1986, when I faced five months in New York without enough stimulation to occupy my mind. My daughter had moved her family into my Cincinnati residence in early May, and I was at loose ends until mid-September, when I would return to the seaside mansion in La Jolla that I rented annually from the movie actor Cliff Robertson.

I therefore took on the new assignment at Printed Matter, while escalating my consulting work with galleries and adding a few artists who wished for me to analyze and promote their careers. These activities helped greatly to brighten my sojourn through the hot, humid summer.

The wife of artist Lawrence Weiner was the director of the organization. I found Alice to be a dear and liked her immediately, but her business and leadership skills were rather undeveloped. The small staff at Printed Matter appeared willing and hard-working, aching for a modicum of guidance.

To her credit, Alice seemed eager to learn, although we could only work together for a couple of hours a day. I would drop by around three in the afternoon and work with her until five. This tiny organization didn't provide much of a challenge to me and, after a thorough diagnosis of the situation, I had a rather easy time getting them on an even keel and stemming the losses that had drained their resources.

When we took an accurate inventory, I found that they had many out-of-print books of considerable value. Printed Matter took pride in selling art books at low prices, often at one or two dollars, which offered a shrewd window of opportunity to adroit middlemen, who would come in and buy an armful, which they would resell for at least fifty dollars apiece. I recall specifically gems by Joseph Beuys, Chuck Close, Gordon Matta-Clark and Douglas Huebler—as well as countless others.

Needless to say, I quickly stopped that practice and repriced everything appropriately. The board members were stunned when I announced at a meeting that Printed Matter had *several hundred thousand dollars* in hidden assets that could eventually be turned into cash.

Printed Matter published a price list with regularity that revealed the rich variety of material it offered, but the customer response was weak, since the staff didn't know the rudiments of marketing. Most importantly, public and university libraries should have purchased each item they offered, but only a handful bought anything at all. (I personally set out to have a collection comprised of all their publications.)

As an experiment, I coughed up a modest sum of money to see if we could expand our customer base. P.M. wrote to major national institutions, making them an introductory offer of $500 worth of books for just $250. Due to the generosity of an anonymous benefactor, P.M. had received a matching grant, provided that an order was placed within thirty days.

An immediate response inundated the mailbox and, for once, the shipping clerk worked overtime to keep up with the orders. I faced the drain of a tidy sum—well beyond what I had originally earmarked—so the board scurried around to find additional donors to alleviate my pain. We had a huge success, and Printed Matter basked in wide publicity.

Other than those two major accomplishments, my intervention consisted of nitty-gritty, pedestrian matters pertaining to the smooth functioning of any organization, all quite easily accomplished. The board expressed their gratitude to me, and one member, artist

Pat Steir, gave me a lovely painting in appreciation. I had plenty of satisfaction helping out, as I interacted with fine people.

When I bowed out of my engagement, I lost contact with P.M. Alice was replaced by someone else, and later they operated under the aegis of the Dominique de Menil Foundation.

Printed Matter moved to spacious quarters on lower Wooster Street, just north of Canal, where I once paid a visit. The space was squeaky clean, with rows of neat racks so that books could be easily identified. A real class act! Yet somehow I felt uneasy in the somewhat sterile atmosphere. All the charm derived from the perennial mess and confusion of a modest storefront had evaporated. Much had been gained, but something important had disappeared forever. I missed Alice very much.

Don Kaufman, Alan Sonfist

Beginning that summer, I started advising two artists about their careers. The first was Don Kaufman, who was much in demand as a "colorist." Unable to make a living as a painter, he had found a special niche in the art world. He worked with eminent architects such as

I. M. Pei, selecting just the right interior and exterior colors for their major building projects, and then supervising the mixture of appropriate hues on-site. Due to his singular talent he was much in demand, and traveled incessantly on the job; but at the end of the year he ended up with little or nothing.

My analysis proved correct: He simply didn't charge enough for his services, since he always feared the architects would desert him if he raised his fees. I urged him to speak candidly with his employers about his problem and come up with a vastly increased hourly rate of pay; he would soon learn if his talent justified it. Magically, his constituents met his "demands" without a whimper, and I hope he lived happily ever after.

The other client was Alan Sonfist, an "ecological" artist, who is famous for a pocket park he developed on the north side of West Houston Street, just east of Sixth Avenue. Alan planted the exact flora that existed when the Indians sold Manhattan to the Dutch, so today we can see a half–city block appear as it must have centuries ago.

I had met Sonfist years earlier when he had an excellent show at Marian Goodman Gallery. His sales then were languishing, which seemed strange since he produced first-class work in a variety of media. He informed me that not only art museums but also natural history museums wanted his output, and he provided me with a long list of prospective buyers. I agreed to mount a campaign in his behalf and see what I could accomplish for him. In return, if I succeeded, I would accept a work of his in recompense instead of a consultant's fee.

Since Alan didn't have a dealer at that time and he had sold his work in the past at good prices, I was able to devise an attractive formula, under which a prospective donor could help an institution by purchasing— and later giving—an object, without cost to himself. Rather skeptical about how Alan had represented the theoretical enthusiasm for his work, I started telephoning specific people whose names he had given, and wrote a slew of masterful sales letters introducing myself as a selfless benefactor of the arts. It all took a lot of my time.

Amazingly enough, the response verified Alan's statements. There were a considerable number of museums who avidly wanted his work and my proposal seemed to make good sense, so directors busied themselves in locating public-spirited citizens. One man in particular, the head of a natural history museum in Albuquerque, said that he had $15,000 in funds available and could make a purchase immediately. He knew Alan personally, respected him and considered him a friend.

When I reported back to Alan, he said he needed a vacation and that New Mexico would be a perfect spot, so he would take transparencies and slides for the director to make his selection; there would be an ideal amalgam of work and pleasure. During our conversation, I gave Alan a rather lengthy follow-up list of what he should provide other interested buyers.

I awaited eagerly news of the sale to Albuquerque. Having heard nothing several weeks after his return to New York, I called Alan to get a report:

"Oh. Bob, I've been meaning to call you, but I've been very busy."

"Well, what happened?"

"Bob, I had a great time, but I couldn't bring up business with a friend and he didn't say anything to me."

I was flabbergasted. Alan Sonfist was his own worst enemy. His extreme passivity and lack of drive or follow-through greatly hampered his career, which should have been brilliant because of his enormous talent.

131

I bowed out of my consulting role gracefully, since there seemed little I could accomplish in Alan's behalf. After years of silence, he telephoned me recently to say hello. He was in San Diego on an assignment and didn't have time to stop by, but wanted to say that he remembered me with affection. He sounded unusually animated, so, hopefully, he is doing splendidly.

Promoting/Supporting the Creative Art World

At times I provided seed money to initiate gallery shows, either because I wanted to further the career of a specific artist or wanted to make art more attractive to the public. Also, I always felt the museums were a bit too inaccessible and snobbish, so I tried to devise ways to entice them into reaching a wider audience. I achieved a few minor wins in the process, noted herewith:

Mary Beebe, the dynamic curator of the Stuart Collection on the campus of the University of California, San Diego, created an outstanding sculpture garden, endowed by a philanthropist named Da Silva. Not long after I moved to La Jolla, she contacted me and suggested that I underwrite a novel project for which no backer could be found. She put me in contact with a new art dealer named Mark Quint, who sought support for his small, storefront gallery in the village.

Mark and his wife, Linda, became close friends. He had a very simple idea, presented to him by the New York artist Moira Sheehan, who was in town. She wanted to take a full-sized telephone pole and place it horizontally straight through his gallery, penetrating the front glass pane and extending through the back wall. It was long enough to leave the ends sticking out of each terminus.

Who could resist such a unique opportunity? Of course I'd be honored to participate. The project was a dazzling success, with lots of laudatory publicity. In the gallery Moira hung estimable drawings that documented her show and I believe they sold very well. (Viewers had to duck under the pole to examine her work.)

Another time I had lunch in Cincinnati with Roberta Lieberman and Victoria Kogan, a partner in TLK Gallery in Costa Mesa, California, who had introduced Roberta and me while visiting in the Midwest. Roberta expressed her displeasure at a temperamental painter who wasn't ready for his one-person exhibit in a

month's time and she had to scour around on short notice for a substitute.

I informed her that I had an ideal answer: Ming Mur-
Ray was an experienced, resourceful artist who could
easily come up with a neat solution; in fact, she had
been eager to do a specific installation at a gallery,
based on a "tennis" motif. Victoria corroborated my
judgment since she knew Ming's work.

By way of background, Ming had been residing in my
carriage house, and the prior summer had done a site-
specific masterpiece on my tennis court. Prior to my departure that July for China, she had told me that driving by my tennis court each day was exceedingly boring
and, with my permission, she'd like to utilize the space
to make a work of art. Since the tennis court needed resurfacing anyway (which I didn't tell her), I assented
readily.

When I returned home from my voyage, I found that
she had painted 600 yellow tennis balls over the entire
playing area. Each, regulation size, had a carefully
drawn seam and was covered with "fuzz." Also, each
ball cast a shadow as though it lay still with the sun low
on the horizon.

Indeed, I had a most unusual tennis court and many

citizens, as well as visiting pros in town for a big tournament, tested their concentration under these odd circumstances. For weeks Ming made a video film of the action and recorded children playing there with wheeled toys as well. The crescendo came when she gave a large "happening" with tables set up around the periphery for guests. She called it "Dining on the Edge," replete with a sound system and blaring music, laser beams fanning through the area, as well as balloons and colored streamers galore. In addition, Ming had television sets installed at the four corners of the tennis court, showing a doubles-match on the new surface, which guests watched while being served Chinese TV dinners.

"Tennis on the Edge" became the title for her lengthy video, eventually well edited, complete with subtitles, computer-composed music and voiceover. It all created quite a stir among the local art cognoscenti who had been participants in the production.

Ming dearly wanted to do a gallery installation, based on her outdoor tennis installation, so, upon Roberta's approval, she went into high gear to ready her show at the Zolle Lieberman Gallery. I find artists incredibly inventive under pressure, digging up resources

135

the ordinary mortal would never dream of. As an example, Ming discovered the Supreme Court Carpeting Company in an obscure Florida village (the name tickled my fancy) which purveyed polypropylene carpeting for all the major professional tournaments in indoor arenas. In exchange for the display of their logo, they would oblige the artist in any way possible!

Prior to installation, Chicago was swamped with mammoth rolls of carpet seconds and scraps, all neatly marked with white lines, and a couple of serviceable—but frayed—tennis nets were thrown into the bargain.

The scene at the opening was quite unique: "Supreme Court" material covered the entire gallery floor, with lines zigzagging in crazy directions. Across the large area were strung several tennis nets at normal height. Strewn around randomly were 250 tennis balls, all colored with bright green or yellow day-glow. In one corner a TV screen ran the film "Tennis on the Edge," and on the walls were stunning oil pastel paintings on paper, depicting various aspects of the "tennis" project.

Guests were encouraged to play with the tennis balls and keep them as souvenirs. Street urchins got the message quickly and throughout the neighborhood youngsters were playing toss after coming in to swipe the balls. That day all the Chicago dealers had simultaneous art openings, but Zolle Lieberman proved to be the public's favorite.

I funded the realization of the installation, not an onerous burden. It pleased me greatly that Ming's drawings sold briskly to sports and art lovers.

On three occasions I instigated shows at the Contemporary Art Center, providing limited funding in each case. (One time I paid for the construction of a new reception desk, an idea vetoed by the CAC board. It caused me a severe reprimand by members for obliging the director—my friend Bob Stearns—against their express wishes.)

One event derived from a request by my new friend, Roberta Lieberman. She had commissioned a number of individual artists to each create a totally novel musical instrument and sought a venue where their handiwork could be shown. Bob Stearns evinced eagerness to have the show, so he booked it for the first opening in his calendar of exhibits at the CAC ("Art Instruments": November 9–December 29, 1984).

The artists all chose to construct percussion instruments that could be strummed, rung, beaten, pounded or plucked. All were sturdily built of wood or metal, some adorned with hide or string, and most were visually quite unusual, even beautiful. Rather than just install a typical museum exhibit of exotic objects, Bob Stearns invited the public to "make music" at the gallery. In a newspaper advertisement, he suggested that Cincinnatians form groups, such as quartets or quintets, and book time at the CAC to perform in ensembles.

Predictably, the response was gratifying and many who had never been inside a museum swarmed downtown to perform. The CAC extended its hours so, night and day, an incredible din arose from the gallery, at times with competing forces, due to an overlapping schedule. Occasionally I would drop in and watch the bedlam, as citizens gleefully unleashed their latent musical talents.

Another show I arranged came about indirectly through the good offices of Diane Waldman, then associate director of the Guggenheim Museum in New York. She commended me to visit the studio of a painter she admired—Scott Davis—whose talent, she felt, was overlooked; she wanted to better expose him to collectors. So I followed her suggestion and met with him. I could tell immediately how correctly Diane had appraised his ability.

While I did not find the artist particularly personable—since he seemed to have a perennial chip on his shoulder—I most definitely wanted to help him. So I bought one painting (*The Eleusinian Mysteries, "Untitled,"* 1978; oil on canvas; 29.8 × 170.2 cm) and shortly afterwards another (*Thinking and Working, "Night Painting,"* 1983; oil on linen; 152.4 × 213.3 cm). Both ended up at the CAM, but in addition I acquired several others that went to the Guggenheim and other institutions.

On that first visit I viewed Scott Davis's magnum opus, *The Annunciation*, a monumental creation in six panels, measuring 9′ × 20′. The work really defies description, but in abstract form it roughly depicts— from left to right—Gabriel's message, Mary's response, Jesus' birth and, finally, the Passion. He had obviously put enormous effort into this giant and suffered the common lament of an artist: He couldn't find a place to show it, so I promised to do what I could in his behalf.

At my suggestion, Bob Stearns visited Davis in New York and agreed immediately to give a show which would highlight *The Annunciation*. Actually, it was a two-person exhibition with Ted Stamm, November 19–December 31, 1982. Scott Davis came to Cincinnati to supervise the installation of his paintings and, in just a few days, managed to antagonize most of the CAC staff with what they charitably referred to as his "anti-social behavior." About that time he wheedled a substantial loan from me, most of which was never repaid.

Years later, Davis sent me an announcement that he was having a show at the Laurie Rubin Gallery and I stopped by to see his recent work. He demonstrated the same great ability I had seen originally; having Ms. Rubin give him an opportunity was a major coup, since she is greatly respected in the art world. I hope he did well.

My great triumph was when Bob Stearns agreed to give Ruby Wilkinson a show November 19–December 31, 1984. Ruby is a retired kindergarten teacher who does fanciful stitchery—usually wall hangings, but also three-dimensional—cleverly utilizing scraps of cloth, braid, buttons and other miscellania to sculpt humans, animals and structures. I met her in 1974 and commissioned her to create specific works based on my ideas for more than a decade. Her detailed, meticulous craftsmanship took so long that I received only thirteen works in all. (I resented it deeply when she gave one to her grandchild.) Some of the subjects were: *The Zoo*, *The Circus*, *Mother Goose* (two panels), *Noah's Ark* and *The Carousel*—as well as *Alice in Wonderland*.

Each year Ruby's handiwork became more complex and wonderful; I kept encouraging her to keep producing and eventually I'd get her a museum show, since she richly deserved one. I had no idea how to execute my commitment; however, I kept pressing Bob Stearns to give Ruby a show at the CAC. Finally, after stalling endlessly, he watched her body of work grow over the years and came to realize that she WAS a great artist.

The CAC exhibit was a success, especially with children, who were bused in from all over the county. It triggered the greatest attendance, greatest new memberships and greatest bookstore sales on record. Ruby, a sprightly Pied Piper, entranced the kids when she gave her "gallery talks and tours" and in her self-effacing way enjoyed the limelight.

Later Ruby's show toured throughout Ohio and the Midwest, ending up at the Smithsonian in Washington. She received the homage I had always wished for her.

Since my principal residence is in La Jolla, I try to be particularly supportive of our local contemporary art museum. Over time I have made numerous art gifts that seem appreciated and, on occasion, I contribute modest sums of money. When Jan Groth had his show, I paid for a simple catalogue that documented the work —rather important for an artist's curriculum vitae.

The director, Hugh Davies, has been gratifyingly open to my sporadic suggestions, which many people in his position might reject out of hand. For instance, he once gave a mini-show to my "toilet paper" collection. He selected choice specimens and ingeniously installed them on a blank wall between the men's and women's restrooms in the rear of a large gallery. They looked really fabulous!

In 1992 Hugh Davies installed a show of Ruby Wilkinson's work, and I paid for school kids to be brought in by bus. Ruby couldn't come to the opening, due to failing health, but in the museum's TV room a taped interview with her, conducted by my daughter Robin, exposed to all the artist's vivacity and incredible charm. Ruby's articulate explanation as to how she constructed her pieces captivated audiences, who crowded the small viewing area and sat spellbound.

4

My Debacle with the Cincinnati Art Museum

In March 1986, the Cincinnati Art Museum had a splendid exhibit of the RSM Collection. Soon afterwards, minor irritants and major violations of my gift agreement culminated in June 1991 with my commencing a lawsuit against the CAM in order to repossess the collection and donate it to another institution more committed to contemporary art.

When I originally embarked on building a contemporary art collection with the express purpose of making a gift to the CAM and thereby attracting a new audience to that institution, I realized there would be major impediments.

My contacts at the museum were tenuous. The previous director, Phil Adams, and his wife, Roseanne, were friends. Phil represented the old school—highly educated, urbane, witty and well versed in antiquities and totally disinterested in art of recent vintage. The chairman of the Board of Trustees until recently, John Warrington, was Phil's worthy counterpart. Although he was knowledgeable about a whole spectrum of fine arts, he never regarded "contemporary" as worthy or indeed as art at all. In fact, when I confessed one evening that I had started collecting contemporary art (although not revealing the motivation), his characteristic snappy and disheartening rejoinder was "Why don't you buy a fine Dürer?"

The incumbent director, Millard Rogers, unlike the previous director and chairman, was devoid of personal charm. A drab personality, he typified the petty bureaucrat. Years before I met him, several staff members—my personal friends—would regale me with anecdotal evidence of his tyrannical ways. Dr. Carol Macht, my intimate friend, served as curator of "pots and pans" (decorative arts). A leading authority in her field, she writhed under the inane constraints and decisions of her boss. As a natural mimic, she would send us into paroxysms as she aped Rogers's Olympian pronouncements. Sometimes Dan Walker, curator of Eastern art, would contribute his favorite "Millard" stories. Sadly, Millard Rogers ruled his fiefdom with an iron fist, terrorizing a fearful staff.

Cincinnatians venerate their art museum as a sacred institution. While its Eastern art collection is outstanding, and there are individual paintings by Mantegna, Botticelli, Cezanne and others—many due to the generosity of the philanthropic Emery family—the museum cannot be compared to those in other major American cities.

Millard Rogers presided over this odd collection. A self-styled authority on early Spanish church art, he had studied under the illustrious John Pope Hennessy —evidently his most transcendent experience. He mesmerized his board, which was mostly composed of important citizens with little knowledge of art. Even John Warrington, normally astute to the point of cynicism, became a devotee of the "Millard cult."

Roughly ten years had elapsed from the time I started the RSM Collection when one day, to my amazement, I received a phone call from Millard Rogers requesting an appointment to visit my art collection and then have lunch. David Reichert, a lawyer for the CAM and board member who kept abreast of my purchases, must have instigated the call. The CAM collection contained a large black sculpture of Louise Nevelson and a wonderful "box" by Donald Judd (formerly at the home of Harriet and Fritz Rauh).* From a generation earlier was a fine Rothko, two huge murals by Joan Miró and Saul Steinberg and a large mobile by Alexander Calder. The last three were donated by the generous Emery family, who had foresightedly commissioned them for the Terrace Plaza Hotel built in the late 1940s.

Rogers took copious notes during his visit and to his credit did not pretend to be knowledgeable about what he saw. We each fled gratefully from an unmemorable lunch. A few weeks later I received a courteous note of thanks in which he cited several works that particularly

---

*Their daughter, while curator at the St. Louis Museum, married the newspaper magnate Joseph Pulitzer, who had a prestigious art collection. Through their joint efforts it grew to a world-class level.

pleased him but must have confused his visit with another, because he named several artists whose oeuvres
I did not own.

In the five years that followed, I remained in contact
with Reichert, who seemed gratifyingly eager for me to
make a major contribution to the CAM, and I postured
myself as a coy maiden being wooed by an ardent
suitor. Meantime, I acquired two allies within the con-
fines of the museum. I met Kristin Spangenberg, curator of all works on paper, who professed a great desire
to acquire my substantial holdings of works eligible for
her department, primarily several hundred prints by Sol
LeWitt, and a goodly number of conceptual photographs. Her department covered such a wide range that
she couldn't do justice to any one specialty, but she tried
valiantly to keep abreast of the contemporary scene.
Blessed with several important endowments, she had
more funds for new purchases than any other curator
and, from time to time, purchased contemporary objects. Unfortunately, Millard seemed to keep her trem-
bling with insecurity.

My second cohort, Denny Young, was an outspoken,
strong-minded woman who was curator of paintings

and sculpture, a title she shared with Rogers, who fancied himself an authority in that area. Denny, a member of the eminent local Taft family, worked diligently for her Ph.D.

Denny knew little about contemporary art, but over a few years having committed herself to a crash course made admirable strides. Unlike other museum personnel, who put down the laity, she absorbed information from whatever source she could tap.

From 1979 to 1984 the RSM Collection had grown exponentially and pressure built to make my gift. Millard Rogers was now actively pursuing me and, in the spring and early summer, we wrote various proposals, culminating in a preliminary contract of understanding between me and the museum on August 1, 1984, with a final version inked on December 8.

The principal clauses of the one-and-a-half-page document were:

1. The CAM would currently allocate for contemporary art galleries 82, 96 and 99, as well as the Terrace Court hallways in the basement.

2. Contemporary art by definition would be

work produced within twenty-five years of acquisition.

3. Beginning in 1986, when the bulk of my collection would have been given, every three years an appraisal would be made, and at least 20 percent of the valuation would be sold off to provide funds for new purchases. At the first appraisal the museum could exclude five works they wished to keep and designate for the permanent collection. Each subsequent triennial, they could exclude three.

4. No new purchases should cost more than $30,000.

5. Deaccessioned objects should be disposed of by auction, consignment to dealers, sales or trade, in order to realize the highest possible price.

6. "It is my primary intent that the museum continually acquire works of contemporary artists and deaccession works that are neither exhibited nor of any importance to the museum's collection."

7. In the event the museum should in the future no longer be interested in contemporary art, it should give the collection to an art museum

149

which is then showing a strong interest in contemporary art (such as the Walker, Albright-Knox, the Chicago Art Institute, etc.).

How I preened when the contract was signed. I had gotten more or less what I wanted. True, I had argued for much more space, anticipating other significant donations, but at least the museum had agreed to two handsome, large galleries, plus more modest space. I felt assured of a mechanism for keeping the collection vibrant while limiting the amount to be spent. This innovation became widely publicized and praised, even by Millard Rogers. I made the gift anonymously, scoffing at proud collectors who insist on plastering their names on museum walls.

Little did I realize that the contract was a worthless document that would never be properly implemented. My enormous conceit precluded my seeking the advice of an attorney, since I assumed that David Reichert represented my interests in his eagerness to have the collection. Only much later in the course of the lawsuit, when I became privy to internal correspondence of the museum, did I become aware of treachery. Through

150

subpoenas and depositions, the true story unfolded and I realized then how foolish a smart man can be.

The contract had been drafted with built-in loopholes permitting the CAM latitude to do more or less what it wished. Ominous signs should have warned me of the museum's tepid commitment to contemporary art. My offer of $150,000 to fund a curatorship for contemporary art to extend over a five-year period was spurned by Rogers, who remarked that he'd only be interested if I made a permanent endowment. (Later I saw internal documents revealing my offer would have disturbed his departmental table of organization.) I also pushed for an "Arts Festival" to be sponsored jointly by the Contemporary Art Center (CAC) and the CAM—a dream my brother-in-law, Charles Westheimer, and I had worked on years earlier. I had revived the idea in the hope of healing a festering rift between the two organizations. I was spurned again.

For two years I fed the CAM the bulk of the RSM Collection, while retaining special favorites for my home in La Jolla. I started sensing a more positive attitude. Toni Birckhead, who has a gallery in Cincinnati, prodded her husband Ollie, CAM board member, to lend support.* Dr. Mary Baskett, owner of a gallery specializing in oriental art, had valuable contacts with the CAM and lent a helping hand. From each I bought selections for the collection, going out of my way to buy the work of local artists, many of whom produced art of high quality. Cole Carothers, Mildred Fischer, Robert Gartzka, Stewart Katz, Ming Mur-Ray and Nellie Taft provide a partial list—it all added up to a network that strengthened my case.

The confluence of positive factors gave impetus to the display of the RSM Collection. Gratifyingly, Denny Young planned a major exhibit for March 1986 and, even better, she opened liaison with the CAC for the planning of my cherished Arts Festival, to occur concurrently with the opening. Millard Rogers finally gave his blessing and for eighteen months we worked cooperatively to achieve an ambitious program.

Through the good offices of Robert Stearns, former director of the CAC, we found outstanding performance artists for our festival. As curator of performing

---

*He was a president of a large bank, the Central Trust Company, that bought impressive works for their main office: a large George Rickey and a marvelous series of monochromatic paintings by Ellsworth Kelly.

arts at the Minneapolis Walker Art Museum, Robert could easily guide us. We arranged for two concerts by Philip Glass at the cavernous Taft Auditorium, as well as shows by San-kai-ju-ku and the Bhutto Group. They would take place on the same weekend as the museum opening, and a week later there would be additional performances. I agreed to fund any deficit, relieving pressure from Denny and her CAC counterpart. Their morale soared.

Invitations went out to various artists, dealers and museum personnel to attend our celebration, and a pleasing number promised attendance. When I queried Rogers as to what hospitality he would offer the out-of-towners, he offered glasses of white wine during the opening. Deeply disappointed—but scarcely surprised—I took matters into my own hands: After the museum opening, I arranged to host a dinner-dance at the downtown Hyatt hotel, with the best in food, booze, music and entertainment. Then various friends rallied and arranged intimate dinner parties prior to the performance nights. Cincinnati would demonstrate elegant Midwest hospitality after all.

When the great week arrived everything exceeded my fondest expectations. Denny Young outdid herself in the difficult job of showing such a wide range of art intelligently. For the first time I saw many paintings and sculptures in a spacious setting, and they looked just wonderful.

The performances, all reasonably sophisticated, demonstrated that Cincinnatians appreciate quality, and, incredibly, we had night after night sell-outs. Best of all Philip Glass drew a capacity crowd both nights. In the end, my contribution to the deficit amounted to a paltry $10,000. I wasn't surprised. Local newspapers had provided advance publicity and gave positive reviews after each event.*

After our brief honeymoon, the CAM and I drifted apart. As I peruse the voluminous documents in my possession, I evidently came off to Rogers and others (not Denny Young) as a quixotic, temperamental know-nothing mercurial rich collector, who constantly meddles in affairs about which he is quite ignorant.

---

*The festival reoccurred a year later without my participation and once again proved highly successful; in fact, it broke even financially. Sadly, according to Denny Young, instead of being an annual or biennial event, it ended, ostensibly because Millard Rogers felt it too distracting a drain on his staff's energies. Without the CAM's sponsorship it no longer became feasible.

Obviously, I don't see myself that way. I try to be self-effacing and undemanding. In actual fact, I would visit far more museums in a year than anyone on the museum staff, and my knowledge of contemporary art was extensive.

About twice a year I would visit Cincinnati, and on each occasion I'd make notes on what I observed at the museum. More often than not I would come unannounced, sometimes informing Rogers's secretary that I was in the building, but telling her not to disturb him if he was busy. Then I might meander about the galleries with Kristin Spangenberg and/or Denny Young. (Only in his deposition did I learn how this habit enraged Millard, who saw me as snooping behind his back.)

On occasion, I would discover highly amusing lapses, at other times some not so funny:

1. I pointed out to Kristin that the galleries seemed incredibly dark and that some ceiling light bulbs needed replacement. Typically defensive, she informed me there were rigid standards regarding light intensity to prevent any degradation of the works on display, and that

galleries were monitored frequently with a light meter. On my next visit, the galleries were definitely brighter. Denny informed me confidentially that after my remark Kristin checked the calibration of the light meter which turned out to be broken.

2. One day, as I strolled about with Denny Young, I pointed out that the galleries resembled a hothouse: large green potted plants, dotted throughout, were obscuring the view of many fine paintings. She whispered that she was well aware of the problem, but I had hit upon an extremely delicate subject. No one had the nerve to address a women's committee of loyal volunteers, whose job was to water and prune.

   With boldness, I wrote my views to Millard and requested the removal of the offensively inappropriate weeds. My mission was accomplished in the contemporary art galleries at the cost of having triggered deep resentment.

3. With frequency I corrected errors in display or mislabeling of art. No one knew enough to be aware of mistakes. Carl Andre's eleven rusty steel plates (which looked great in my office, but

rather pathetic in a large room) should have
been installed in a single row with the widths
touching. Instead, the piece was installed
lengthwise, more or less in a "Z" pattern.

Douglas Huebler had come expressly to Cincinnati
to rehabilitate a sculpture dating from the 1960s which
needed repair. He worked at the museum, leaving a dia-
gram indicating correct installation. Ignoring instructions, it was installed upside down. Next to this piece,
in a mini-exhibition space off the main lobby, was a
stunning head and upper torso of an arrogant woman,
sculpted by Italo Scanga. The label read "Portrait of
Robert Orton"!*

A painting of Lynton Wells was hung upside down;
I admit that, in this instance, it didn't actually look that
bad.

In the years that followed the illustrious RSM exhibit,
fewer and fewer objects from our collection were displayed. I would write a note to Millard Rogers, giving

*I had wanted to keep this great sculpture for myself, but Denny Young
talked me out of it; a few years later Christie's misappraised it low at $7–
10,000 and it was deaccessioned and sold there for $1200, a price I would
have gladly paid.

him head counts. The galleries designated for contemporary art continued to display work created well before the twenty-five years called for in the contract. Although some, such as the Miró mural and the Rothko, represented key former acquisitions, they still displaced more recent art that I would like to have shown. It had been my fervent desire for my gift to attract other collectors to follow an example, so it would have pleased me to see better or more important art hung. When we wrote the contract such intent was explicitly expressed. To my horror, I saw execrable paintings supplanting RSM gems that remained in the basement storage area. I admit to strong opinions in the matter of aesthetics and someone else can have a different view, but I would shudder to see oils by Miriam Schapiro and Peter Huttinger, as well as a boring tondo by Rodney Ripps, all gifts or promised gifts to the CAM. Obviously Rogers catered to the wrong donors while he seriously and unalterably alienated the museum's most important potential benefactor.

I have mentioned elsewhere my admiration for the unerring taste of Douglas Cramer, who has built perhaps the finest contemporary art collection in the United States. A Cincinnatian by birth, he was well dis-

158

posed to his hometown (although dwelling in L.A.) and had on occasion lent masterpieces to the museum. Denny Young nurtured a relationship that seemed to be bearing fruit, since Cramer indicated the possibility of making a major contribution in memory of his mother, and would pay for redecorating galleries that would contain the work.

The disaster that ensued I've heard mainly from Denny. As a quid pro quo, Doug requested her to mount an exhibit of some major works, all on rather short notice, which would obviate his storing the paintings while his *second* private museum was being refurbished. She rallied museum crews to the cause and came up with a plausible plan that would oblige the incipient angel.

Cramer was more than pleased at the cooperation and said he would fly into Cincinnati to finalize details. At that point Denny proudly presented Millard Rogers with her outstanding coup, but to her consternation the director reacted with rage that anyone could expect such special treatment. If Cramer wanted a show, he could have one planned well ahead in orderly fashion. When the great collector arrived in town he found the director too busy to keep the luncheon engagement and, upon hearing Denny's weak excuses, he left the city, swearing never to deal again with the museum.

When Denny informed me of what happened I foolishly volunteered to contact certain key board members to see if we might possibly salvage the relationship. I telephoned several men but in each case found unwavering support for Millard. As a result of Denny Young's flagrant insubordination, she was dismissed from her position, leaving a void. Her dismissal showed the lack of commitment to contemporary art.

Her replacement, John Wilson, a courteous gentleman, is a medievalist, I believe, and, with becoming modesty, claimed no expertise in the current art scene, so that left only Kristin, who has a specialized knowledge of contemporary prints and photographs.

When the contract was first negotiated, I fought hard to expand the galleries enumerated specifically for contemporary art. Secretly I sympathized with Rogers's dilemma: It was a general museum with a wide spectrum to present, so compromises had to be made. Yet I was assured that before long all the galleries would be renovated and rehung chronologically. At that time it would be appropriate to add additional space; so I had to content myself with that empty promise.

Rooms contained acres of mediocre paintings and ghastly sculptures. If only Rogers would concentrate on my specialty, the museum would become nationally noticed. It made sense to me that they emulate the "East Wing" to gain a reputation.

One small victory was the designation of the so-called Terrace Court area in the basement for the display of contemporary art. Although stuck in a low traffic zone, there was great available wall space. Denny and principally Kristin did a credible job of installation there.

In 1988, I noted that all the art had been replaced by posters. I wrote a letter to Rogers, reminding him of our contract terms and requesting reinstallation of contemporary art in the appropriate area. (With diminished display in the other galleries, contemporary art was fast disappearing.) Months passed without a reply; but after further prodding I got my answer: It had been decided that the light levels were inappropriate for the installation of art and, furthermore, the traffic in that area caused by visitors to the restaurant and audito-

161

rium was so heavy that there was a grave danger of works being damaged. He suggested a substitution: a balcony area above the main lobby, which he claimed had roughly the same running feet of walls.

I demurred at his suggestion, since the balcony was dark and low ceilinged. Firmly I asked the museum to live up to the agreement, adding that if any damage might occur I would free them of any responsibility. I never received an answer to this letter. This breach later became one among many important charges in my lawsuit.

During Millard Rogers's deposition in October 1991, he cited the opinions of all his in-house experts at the rectitude of his decision, totally ignoring the central point. He eloquently defended his position but, interestingly enough, as the trial date loomed ahead, the Terrace Court once again contained a full quota of contemporary art.

This last demonstration of contempt started me on the road to repossessing the RSM Collection, to find for it a more hospitable home outside of Cincinnati, since I couldn't think of an alternate site.

In June 1989, Jay Chatterjee, the highly competent dean of DAA (the design, art and architectural school) at the University of Cincinnati, paid me a visit in La Jolla.

Jay understood my frustration, but beseeched me to consider some way to keep the work in Cincinnati. As a board member of the Contemporary Art Center, he felt that if I would pledge the collection to that institution he might be able to persuade his board to expand the CAC's activities, which would certainly entail enlarging their limited exhibition space as they embarked in a new direction. I responded enthusiastically to his suggestion, stating that I had originally wanted the CAC to have my purchases but they declined, as they were then in no position to accept a large donation.

Chatterjee returned home and met with the dynamic director of the CAC, Dennis Barrie, who favored our plan; but he wanted to make sure that there would be no escalation in the bad blood between his group and the CAM. I assured him that if he didn't accept my treasures they would leave the city, and *that* was a firm resolve.

With the help of my friend and attorney, Bob Brown, I sent a letter to Millard Rogers stating that our contract had been violated and there was obviously not a commitment on the part of the CAM to the proper dis-

163

play of contemporary art. So I wished to move the art to another venue—specifically the CAC.

In the ensuing months Bob Brown negotiated in my behalf, dealing mainly with Jack Schiff, chairman of the Board of Trustees of the CAM. The latter appeared sympathetic to my position, and together they crafted a compromise wherein selected works of art would remain at the museum and the balance would be transferred to the CAC. At the final moment, when Bob and I were rather certain the agreement would be consummated, Schiff telephoned to La Jolla to report reluctantly that the CAM board had vetoed the plan, hinting that it was due to the recalcitrance of an anonymous board member. I warned him that if I had no alternative but to enter a lawsuit to accomplish my goal, the ensuing publicity would damage the CAM's reputation—at a time of a major fund-raising campaign for capital improvements.

In the next several years, board members tried to settle the matter amicably, but each time some malign hand neatly blocked its effectuation. From the time the newspapers announced the lawsuit, I received flak from the community. One *did not* sue such an august icon of the Queen City! My sister, May, was particularly horrified at her brother's aberrant action. I had obviously violated all norms of civilized behavior. Until the final settlement of the case, I never spoke of what caused my action, since I had no desire to harm the reputation of the CAM.

Everyone misunderstood my motives, except for a loyal coterie in the local art community who cheered my efforts. At one point a CAM board member, whom I knew rather well, telephoned me in California begging me to withdraw my suit; in the same breath he stated that the CAM wished to give a ball for me to honor my public-spirited accomplishments. I thought this thinly veiled bribe pretty funny; the man totally misread me, since the last thing in the world I'd want would be such tawdry publicity; I always had carefully kept philanthropy anonymous. He felt he had offered a plum that could not be refused and was startled when I summarily refused his offer.

In January 1990, after learning that Christie's had made an appraisal of the RSM Collection, I requested Rogers to supply a copy, which he sent off immediately. This first step in the triennial cycle of appraisal, de-accession, sale and eventual fresh purchases of art was obviously far behind schedule. Considering that the final gifts were made in early 1986, the process was at least a year late. In adversarial circumstances it provided another serious breach of contract. Still, during the first half of that year I clung to the vain hope that matters could be settled in friendly fashion, so the tardiness didn't alarm me.

But what *did* alarm me mightily was the handiwork of Christie's, which clearly revealed an almost total lack of knowledge of the contemporary art market. Except for a handful of full prices, page after page contained absurd valuations. To give a smattering of examples, listed on page 1 was a large painting by Gary Bower; estimate: $1,200 (later sold for $30). Bower had a one-man show a few years earlier at the Cleveland Center for Contemporary Art and this painting was on the cover of the catalogue. Later, when I queried the director about that specific painting, she said if she had known it might be available she felt she could have raised $18,000 to purchase it for their permanent collection.

On page 2 another large painting by Christopher Brown had also an estimate of $1,200 (later sold for $30). In her deposition on December 3, 1991, Roberta B. Lieberman, Brown's Chicago dealer, stated that she could have sold the oil for $40,000–50,000 since he was a "hot" artist who produced work very slowly. Of course, she was sick that she didn't know about the auction at the Chicago Leslie Hindman Auctioneers, which she could have easily attended if she had known about it. (Hers was a typical response from the art community, which missed out on roughly $350,000 worth of art. Fifty-three items went for $1,100—approximately $20 apiece!)

A third example should suffice: On page 30 of the appraisal a photograph by Richard Long, entitled *A Circle in Africa*, had an estimate of $200, while a price of $30,000 might not have been an exaggerated amount. It had been shown at the Stedlijk Museum in Amsterdam and appeared on the cover of its catalogue. Mercifully the CAM failed to dispose of this jewel.

My blood pressure rose thumbing through the Christie's appraisals and I telephoned various dealers who had originally sold me the art. In those days of soaring prices I didn't keep well abreast, but it didn't take long to find out that the listed estimates were flagrantly wrong. Repeatedly, gallery owners assured me that if the CAM would give them the opportunity they could obtain splendid prices, while making handsome profits themselves. Several said they would be happy to handle a transaction for a 20 percent profit, roughly the same as an auction house.

After a lot of work I came to the conclusion that a fairly accurate appraisal of the RSM Collection would be well over $5,000,000 instead of $2,162,400, which was Christie's estimate. With this information in hand, I telephoned Millard Rogers to inform him of my investigation and conclusions. I forcefully emphasized that it would be disastrous to put the deaccessioned material in the hands of a New York auction house; instead I'd gladly lend a hand to see that the proper parties disposed of the art in a sane and orderly fashion when the museum had decided just what they wished to deaccession and sell.

Ours was a long conversation, during which I gave numerous specific facts to reinforce my argument. He received my information courteously but without comment, and I emphasized my availability to the CAM if they wished my assistance in the future. This particular dialogue became exceedingly important much later in strengthening our case.

In May 1990 my cousin Anne Rorimer came to Cincinnati for a meeting with the CAM who, at my suggestion, had hired her as a consultant for deaccession. Anne's input was largely ignored. She commented on the startlingly low appraisal by Christie's and, as a result, the staff revised the aggregate upward by roughly $300,000. Anne would be the first to admit a lack of thorough knowledge of the art market. She told me later that she merely corrected flagrant errors based on recent sales.

By coincidence, I happened to be in Cincinnati during Anne's stay, and one night we went to Millard Rogers's home for dinner. He had invited a group of citizens interested in contemporary art, with the intention of forming some museum committee. After a pleasant dinner, my first (and last) at his house, he gave a pretty speech during which he announced that most of the museum galleries would be shut down for a couple of years. A multimillion-dollar renovation would pretty well gut much of the building, after which it would be restored to its former glory. Of course, this entailed closing all the second-floor rooms that contained the RSM Collection.

Hearing the news this way left me shocked. As an important donor I felt that I should have been informed earlier. Couldn't accommodation have been made to display some contemporary art in the galleries that remained open? More than ever I became resolved to sever relations with the CAM.

Valiantly, Bob Brown renewed efforts to remove the RSM art from the CAM, since none would be displayed for years. For the next twelve months, we came close to achieving our goal, only to have negotiations break down at the last minute.

In late May 1991, I learned through the grapevine that during the last month the CAM had sold a number of works from the RSM Collection at auction; so I requested Rogers, through my attorney, to supply me with the information. When the list arrived I felt nauseous; the results had been disastrous. Immediately I had a meeting with Bob Brown and instructed him to commence a lawsuit against the CAM for removal of the RSM Collection.

I informed Bob Brown that I had trapped myself into an untenable position. I felt personally responsible for what had happened to many of my friends in the art world who had sold me their art in good faith and had been grievously betrayed by the CAM's irresponsible act. The careers of many wonderful artists might be

170

wrecked as word got out about what had occurred. Reputable dealers would have their livelihood impaired, for, in this computerized age, all auction prices are automatically tracked and published.

As word of the auction sales leaked out in the art community, I received universal approbation for my course of action. For too long everyone had accepted unsavory symbiosis between auction houses and museums, so damaging to dealers and artists as well as collectors.

When Bob and I first sat down to review the merits of our case against the museum he pointed out a serious flaw. The first paragraph of the contract stated: "The Museum will currently allocate for contemporary art galleries 82, 96 and 99 etc. . . ." While I had assumed that "currently" meant "permanently" or "continuously," Bob pointed out that a legal interpretation would be quite different. So, predictably, in the museum's response to our complaint, it claimed the right to display contemporary art as it deemed fit, beyond an undefined "current" period of time. Of course, all correspondence and conversations prior to the contract showed a different interpretation, yet it remained a

171

sword of Damocles to weaken our case. (When we subpoenaed the museum's internal correspondence it became abundantly clear that the treacherous word had been inserted on purpose, to give the CAM a handy escape clause.) Still, we had plenty of other grounds for showing breach of contract and, more importantly, the CAM's lack of commitment to contemporary art.

The CAM showed surprising resourcefulness. Just a week after we filed suit, the CAM issued a press release announcing the appointment of a curator of contemporary art—a timely demonstration of the institution's commitment. Obviously, Rogers knew litigation was pending and I had to admire this belated master stroke. He actually made a felicitous choice. Jean Feinberg, who didn't know of the pending suit or that most of the art she was to curate might be removed, was well respected in New York.

During the summer of 1991 we received cartons full of CAM documents; some proved so damaging to its cause that I marveled at the candor; in its place I'd have conducted a shredding party!

The discovery process escalated with a series of depositions from October 15, 1991, until February 4, 1992.

I most enjoyed the two-day deposition of Millard Rogers, as his cool facade crumbled. Beforehand, several people who knew him well provided sage advice: Two dominant traits should be kept in mind. First, he had a horrible memory. Second, he was a master at disinformation, constantly contradicting himself.

In the course of two days there were hours of "parry and thrust" and I still savor the first day Bob Brown mildly brought up the conversation I had with Millard after receiving the Christie's auction estimates. I had warned Rogers of the document's inaccuracy, and subsequently offered assistance in the disposal of deaccessioned objects. Rogers, sensing a time bomb, coyly admitted that the conversation might have taken place, but he had absolutely no recollection.

But the subject did unleash a passionate tirade. If Orton had interfered with gratuitous advice it would be typical of him—an amateur dabbling in matters best left to professionals. Despite the various options suggested in the contract, Rogers knew full well that the *only* way to dispose of works from a museum was by public auction—an open forum, where free market forces operated. Even when Brown cited many examples of the pittance obtained at Leslie Hindman's (ac-

173

tually less than the cost of packing and shipping), as opposed to the testimony of dealers, he stubbornly stuck to his guns.

On the second day, in midmorning, Bob Brown returned slyly to my January "Christie's" conversation. Casually assuming that Rogers recalled our talk, he started discussing the substance of our chat. To my astonishment, the director said he clearly remembered what had transpired and saw no reason to take seriously the suggestions proffered, as he knew exactly what steps to take through long experience.

This delicious tidbit was just one of many inconsistencies in Rogers's testimony. It would have been interesting indeed to have heard Bob Brown examine him on the witness stand during the course of the trial.

The documents subpoenaed from Leslie Hindman Auctioneers and the depositions of her and her staff were particularly fascinating. The former registrar of the CAM and, subsequently, an employee of Leslie Hindman Auctioneers sought financial backing in December 1990 from Leslie Hindman for a business proposal and then began to discuss working for her permanently. In February 1991, she consigned roughly fifty RSM works (rejected by Christie's) to LHA and, that same month, had another meeting with Hindman. The auction occurred April 14 and 15; the pathetic proceeds were remitted to the CAM on May 14. The registrar accepted employment with LHA at the end of May, and informed the museum on June 5.

At no time prior to her resignation was the museum cognizant of the registrar's negotiations with Hindman. She alone arranged the auction and approved placement of the RSM art in AN AUCTION OF HOUSEHOLD EFFECTS, INCLUDING KITCHEN CABINETS, AN "EXERCYCLE" AND A BUMPER POOL TABLE! When Hindman noted on the list submitted for sale exceedingly low prices (not radically different than the actual results), the registrar somehow failed to contact anyone at the CAM to seek a better disposition. As Kristin Spangenberg commented, "Prices realized in some cases [were] ridiculous. Frame worth more."

Bob Brown forced a reluctant Hindman to supply the names and addresses of the auction bounty. Over Hindman's strenuous objections we contacted a number of the recipients, who were mostly antique shops and "auction junkies," in an effort to retrieve the RSM art. With only one exception, we faced a strange stone wall. None of the buyers had anything for sale. We tantalized them with the idea that they would reap thousands in profit after an outlay of peanuts. How do you buy back a painting worth $40,000 or more from someone who paid roughly $30? (Stewart Katz bought back most of his paintings from a down-state man, who garnered a handsome profit. Afterwards Katz in turn resold the works to collectors, gaining thousands of dollars in the process.)

We learned that the staff of Leslie Hindman had bought a number of works, as did Hindman herself, for little or nothing. According to my acquaintance, Barney Oscher, owner of Butterfield and Butterfield, a reputable auction house in San Francisco, this was a clear violation of the ethical standard of auctioneers.

These events showed a clear-cut conflict of interest. In fact, I felt strongly that the CAM should enter a lawsuit against Leslie Hindman for substantial damages. However, even after the departure of Millard Rogers as director and a new president and chairman of the board of the CAM were installed, no one has seen fit to pursue the matter.

176

When Christie's auctioned off a paltry number of RSM items, the results were quite different. The museum netted roughly $35,000; by my estimate that was perhaps 30 percent of what it might have received through dealer sales. A number of items failed to reach the reserve price. I managed to reconstruct what had happened. I can't place blame on Christie's, who had issued a veiled warning to the CAM. But I do fault them for accepting *any* of the RSM art for auction after reading a letter to Millard Rogers dated November 8, 1989, from Jay Cantor, Christie's senior vice president and director of Museum Services.

He says, with pardonable salesman's prerogative: "I have spoken to Susan Dunne, head of the contemporary department, and she is most enthusiastic about this project" (i.e., appraisal and sale). Yet later in the paragraph he writes: "Susan will be in the best position, not only to provide valuations, but to suggest what is especially strong in the present market, and which works need further market maturity." (Obvious answer: Nothing would be eligible!)

In the autumn of 1991, I made the acquaintance of Susan Dunne, who had recently become director of the downtown space of Pace Gallery. Angela Westwater arranged the impromptu introduction and I caught Susan unaware; so she found herself attacked by an irate Orton over the horrendous appraisal by Christie's. To her great credit, she conducted herself with estimable dignity, while explaining that the CAM had not received an appraisal, as I understood the word; instead, although the title read "Insurance Appraisal," it was actually a conservative pricing of what Dunne felt might be received at auction. Upon my request, she expanded on her remarks in a letter of October 4, 1991, in which she said:

"It was a pleasure to meet you yesterday. I write now regarding the appraisal done by Christie's for The RSM Company Collection.

"First off, this is what is known as a 'fair market valuation,' reflecting the current high and low market figures for the artists listed. Generally speaking, auction estimates are usually 50 percent to 75 percent of retail. The terms 'NSV' and 'VSV' are translated as 'No Sale Value' or 'Very Small Value.'*

"I understand your concern that many of the estimates seem low, or are less than the retail prices that

---

*The appraisal contained a lot of NSVs and VSVs, including almost all LeWitt prints.

could be attained by the artists' dealers. Speaking from the point of view of the Contemporary Art Department at Christie's, these are not works that we would have encouraged for sale at auction. Works by artists who have never come up at auction and who do not have an extremely active primary market and a strong international reputation are difficult to sell on the secondary market. They can only be offered on a decorative basis and this can be damaging to the public perception of the artist. By giving you very low estimates, the auction house is pointing out that this is the best they feel they can obtain for you and they are not encouraging the business. These pieces would be best sold privately by the dealers from whom you purchased them.

"On another note, the works of art which have been given healthy estimates would probably be best sold at auction. The auction process creates a competitive bidding situation which can enable a piece to achieve a higher price than it would on the primary market."

To my mind, Susan Dunne is honest and stated the case eloquently. Auctions are basically theater and only when there is a dramatic situation with fiercely competing avaricious buyers do the results justify the choice. RSM had few, if any, works of art that would have been suitable under her definition. When the CAM selected five works to exclude from sale, they accounted for almost exactly half the appraisal Christie's supplied. Those by Clemente, Fischl, Judd, LeWitt, as well as Gilbert and George, amounted to an estimate of $1,245,000, and the balance of the collection, $1,223,180. Indeed, I'm not convinced that even these five would have fared well.

In summary, under our contract, based on the stipulated 20 percent of the appraised value to be sold, the amount would have been $244,000—and that would be after a falsely low figure. So, quite clearly, it would have been impossible to glean such a sum at any auction house. The only plausible answer would have been to follow my original suggestion regarding disposition and, thereby, according to contract, "obtain the best possible price."

The CAM has two glib rationalizations for the disaster. With some validity, it cited the weakening prices for all art; but if works had been sold in timely fashion, as called for in the contract, prices would have been incredibly stronger. The second defense appears in their internal memoranda: "Due to the quirky nature of Orton's taste, most of the artists he chose were quickly out of fashion." This is patently false in the main; many of the artists I selected have gained higher stature in the years that followed.

An enigma remains unresolved: Why did the CAM fight so hard to retain a collection it regarded so poorly? Or, conversely, why did it handle our agreement so shamefully if they appreciated my gift?

The story ended suddenly, just two weeks before we were to go to trial. By that time both sides were financially drained, with worse to come.

Many months before, Dennis Barrie had been ruthlessly dismissed as director of the Contemporary Art Center. Apparently this action stemmed from his courageous stance in the infamous "Mapplethorpe Trial."*

I had become a close friend of Dennis and his wife, Diane, and publicly supported him during his crisis. At that time Millard Rogers and the CAM were practi-

---

*The trial received international publicity, when Barrie faced a possible jail sentence for displaying certain homo-erotic photographs deemed obscene. To the infinite credit of a jury of ordinary citizens, he was acquitted on all counts. Because of this he became idolized by many Americans as a folk hero, while reviled by many of the power structure of Cincinnati, who evidently got their revenge.

cally alone among prominent American art institutions in not rallying to his defense. Their silence was deafening and reprehensible, so it would have given me exquisite pleasure to have the RSM Collection transferred to the CAC, not only for valid artistic reasons, but also as a bold statement regarding my loyalties.

When Barrie departed, the grandiose but feasible plans for the CAC to accept our works of art collapsed immediately. In fact, for over a year no one from the CAC ever contacted me, quite understandably because no new permanent director had been appointed. With the CAC in such disarray, quite obviously that would not be the venue for our collection. Mistakenly I had not made overtures to another museum, which could have produced an immediate willingness to receive an important gift. An option might have been the Wexler Museum in Columbus, Ohio, where Bob Stearns was the director. That would have been a delicious move, since Stearns, himself, had been unfairly dismissed when director of the CAC.

Other factors weakened my obdurate position. Jean Feinberg was a splendid choice for curator of contemporary art at the CAM. She established a cordial relationship with me sub rosa, and I would have liked to be in a position to help her. A sixth sense gave me the impression that she was less than happy with the support given by her director, but she was in no position to voice any concerns to me under awkward circumstances. Finally, I heard whispers that Millard Rogers would not be director for much longer.

These then were the determinants that caused me to relent and agree to a settlement. We scrapped the original agreement as being unworkable. Then I extracted an admission that the CAM had indeed violated our agreement. Next, they reimbursed me $25,000 to help cover a fraction of my legal fees. They permitted me to make any final decision regarding future deaccession and sales, as well as the right to give approval for any new purchases of contemporary art. This meant that I would control the spending of roughly $40,000 already in their coffers and, in the future, the RSM Collection could not be emasculated without my permission. At my death, understandably, the rights allotted to me would revert to the CAM.

I felt that I could have extracted substantially more money from the CAM, since the direct cost of further litigation would have been a fortune, but the adverse publicity would have cost even more, as confidence in

183

the institution would be badly shaken. Most of all, I wanted to make a point, and not be too punitive with Cincinnati's cherished museum. One item included in our agreement was a perpetual ban against the museum's use of Leslie Hindman Auctioneers for disposal of contemporary art.

In our negotiations a lot of time was spent in the drafting of a press release. I wanted something that would permit my sister to hold her head high once again in the community, and remove the blot on the family escutcheon caused by an erratic brother. That entailed a low-keyed admission of contract violation by the CAM, and notice that I had been reimbursed a token sum by way of damages.

Both sides gave the identical press release to the local papers simultaneously, and I waited for days to see a squib in print; yet unsurprisingly nothing was forthcoming. Finally, a brief announcement appeared in the morning *Enquirer* to the effect that J. Robert Orton Jr. had dropped his lawsuit versus the CAM. Such is the unseen power of our local institutions.

Epilogue: Rogers retired in the autumn of 1994, although he remains a consultant to the museum. Barbara Gibbs, former director of the Sacramento Museum, replaced him. Bearing impressive credentials, she is obviously a "people person" to whom the staff respond with honesty. She immediately faced a substantial budgetary deficit inherited from her predecessor, and early on she eliminated many superfluous administrative posts, correctly placing additional responsibilities with the curators.

Gibbs and several board members have met with me in an effort to mend fences. I've told them I am amenable to resuming my gifts at any future time when Millard Rogers has severed all connections with the CAM. Yet, despite this firm resolve, ashamedly I must confess that in December 1994 I contributed $15,000 to the CAM for the acquisition of art. The bulk of it went for the purchase of a fine painting by my friend Andy Spence.

5

La Jolla Garden Sculpture

". . . if you had not been expelled from the noble castle by hard kicks in your backside for love of Mademoiselle Conegonde, if you had not been clapped into the Inquisition, if you had not wandered about America on foot, if you had not stuck your sword in the Baron, if you had not lost all your sheep from the land of Eldorado, you would not be eating candied citrons and pistachios here."
"Tis well said," replied Candide, "but we must cultivate our gardens."

VOLTAIRE

My home is rather small and the rooms have somewhat low ceilings, so I have resisted any purchases for the interior. The *exterior* is another matter: Since I own just shy of three acres, and there are thirty acres of public hillside abutting the eastern boundary, I can give free rein to my acquisitive instincts for outdoor sculpture.

The property, viewed from the air, resembles an hourglass, with better than an acre at each extremity, while in the middle is situated the main residence and a swimming pool. The house fits snugly against a steep slope and the pool is perhaps sixty feet from the neighbor's driveway. Providing privacy is a gigantic Eugenia hedge, easily thirty feet high, that runs along the property line in the central portion.

La Jolla is laced with canyons, and I reside in one, a cul-de-sac well hidden from the outside world—although right in the middle of the suburb. Since land prices are astronomically high, the former owner had converted a gully into usable space with vast quantities of landfill. The conversion created a mini-paradise, rich with shrubbery and flowers, all of which grow spectacularly in the semitropical climate and bloom all year long, offering bright splotches of purple and red bougainvillea, competing with azaleas (which bloom twice a year), gardenias, and camellias of varying hues. (Often the camellias grow as tall as trees, thirty feet high.)

While a visitor may not be consciously aware of the topography, the land really consists of a series of tiers that descend gradually down the wadi, eventually leveling out into a wide expanse. At this far end is a separate back entrance, connected to a totally different street than the one at the main gate. (This proved a godsend when heavy elements and sculptures had to be unloaded and placed in that area.)

Because of chronic water shortage in Southern California, the various lawns are limited in size, although in the lower garden one is about a quarter acre. Other areas have myrtle, ivy and ice plants as ground cover. On the slopes the ice plants deter erosion, a constant threat at the advent of torrential deluges of rain. There are some sixty fruit trees (mainly citrus, but also fig, apricot, loquat, peach, apricot, apple), a half-dozen avocado, almond, and several varieties of towering eucalyptus trees.

Dotted about this landscape are twenty-odd sculptures, placed in helter-skelter fashion, as I consciously avoid any semblance of formality. In contrast to Storm King Sculpture Park in Cornwall, New York, my purpose is to have a visitor enjoy a sense of discovery by wandering about and finding art in less than obvious sites.

Since 1986 I have been adding roughly three objects annually, although there has been no formula. Indeed the garden has developed ad hoc, with most purchases made on impulse. I had the vague idea of inviting sculptors whom I knew and respected to make something site-specific. Most of them have never had a private commission, since they are accustomed to projects for cities, schools, government bodies or museums. This often entails submitting detailed proposals and accurate budgets, often in competition with other artists— an enervating, time-consuming, frequently unrewarding activity.

I hoped that my approach would provide a refreshing change of pace: I would invite an artist to visit the property, select a location, develop a specific idea and submit it for final approval. As a committee of one, I would give approval expeditiously, without customary bureaucratic red tape or public hearings. If the artist constructed the sculpture "in situ," I offered a comfortable

189

guest house, an extra automobile to use, and the meals of an excellent chef. These temptations proved alluring to some, although in several cases not with any sense of urgency. Since the artists had other priorities and commitments, the usual time span from gestation to completion ranged from two to three years. Usually I would have a number of prospective plans in the wings, since there was such a lengthy lead time.

Since public art could be infinitely more lucrative (if cost estimates were accurate), I understood why I would always be on a back burner, fitting into the schedule of a busy artist as a convenient moment arose. Actually, only 50 percent of the pieces were designed specially for my garden; these involved a major thrust by all parties and a large dose of patience and forbearance on my part. I always wanted it to be a pleasurable experience for both the sculptor and myself, so I was determined to act with insouciance, willing to face the cognitive dissonance which is the trait of many artists. I saw process almost as important as final outcome and usually each project was documented photographically from beginning to end.

At the outset, most sculptures came into being more

or less as a favor, based on an earlier friendship with the artist. Later, artists I didn't know acquiesced rather readily, since they liked the company they would be keeping. They wanted to join others whom they respected, none of whom were exactly household names, but rather artists' artists. At no time did I buy expensive works by a Di Suvero or Moore, but rather by those with a solid reputation in the art world or from others relatively obscure. Several had fine reputations in Europe but were virtually unknown in the United States.

Since often the construction of sculptural pieces is far more expensive than producing a painting (i.e., casting bronze), I discarded my former budgetary guidelines and greatly escalated my annual expenditure. Also, I realized that artists were not exactly efficient cost accountants, so I made allowances for possible deficiencies and always mentally added 10 to 20 percent of an estimate for cost overruns. Little did I imagine how woefully inadequate this sum would be.

For some years no singular setback would faze me. I relished being part of the creative process in the role of a California Medici. I rejoiced with the artists upon the completion of a complex project, proud to see the results upon fruition. But now, older and wiser, I have changed my stance radically. My unalloyed pleasure has turned to dust, as I have been assailed repeatedly by artistic temperament, which left both parties limp, unhappy and exhausted. I've taken the pledge never again to commission a site-specific work. Instead, I am willing to purchase specific prefabricated sculpture that I can plop on a plot of ground, preferably a work by an artist whom I don't know. I speak a bit hyperbolically, since I have made a few purchases recently from artist friends, but these works had already been constructed and their placement in the yard presented no problem.

As a further precaution, I have begun avoiding any sculptures involving *moving* parts: I inhibit any impulse to buy "kinetic" art that necessitates electricity and, even more importantly, water pieces that entail pumps and circulation systems. Trying to keep all systems operative can become a nightmare. I have a monthly contract with "The Pond Doctor" (seriously, his corporate name) who services my garden and the various San Diego civic fountains. At times even *that* specialist is stumped, and I call in a master electrician who knows the vagaries of my most obstreperous water sculptures. Parenthetically, none of this comes cheap!

I confess that I've derived a lot of satisfaction from the garden, and somehow the individual scattered selections now add up to a reasonably coherent whole. Probably I shall continue muddling along in my usual manner, as there is still a lot of space available.

Joel Fisher

I first saw artist Joel Fisher's work in 1982 at Nigel Greenwood Gallery in London, where a number of fine bronze figurines on a display shelf caught my attention. Somehow I was distracted and didn't purchase them, but they lingered in my mind even a year later, when I returned and learned that all the work had been sold in the interim. Joel Fisher had moved back to New York after living in England and Germany for six years. Nigel informed me that Joel and his infant son, Noah, were living in abysmal poverty on The Bowery, and that it would be a great personal favor if I would look him up and perhaps assist him in some way.

Nigel had not exaggerated: I found Joel living on the second floor of a seedy tenement, trying to sculpt and take care of a child in one medium-sized room. I don't know how he was staying alive, but I saw that he could certainly use some help. I recognized his great ability and immediately like him. Despite his adversity, he still had a warm, self-deprecating sense of humor. At that first meeting I offered to give Joel $500 per month in exchange for supplying me with his undetermined artistic output.

Joel was not a stranger to the New York art scene. He had started showing with Paula Cooper, switched to Sonnabend, and ended up with Max Protetch—all fatal moves for a young artist who gained the reputation of being exceedingly talented, yet disloyal and unreliable. I never heard the details, but I know he rued those youthful follies, which hampered his career when he sorely needed a gallery.

The next year I mentioned Joel's plight to my friend Italo Scanga, who was serving on the advisory board of the National Endowment for the Arts. Italo knew, liked and respected Joel and arranged for a $10,000 grant, which really made a huge difference and marked a turning point in his life. Shortly after that Joel started showing with Diane Brown, and not much later was blessed by a front half-page spread in the Sunday *Times* Arts and Leisure section, which lauded his ability.

The prestige that redounded from that single article astounded me, as it launched a thriving career. Joel immediately started to receive substantial sums for his major works in bronze, and good prices for cunning works on paper that he hand-molded. Before long he was earning a handsome living, could afford a large studio along the East River, and built another in northern Vermont near the Canadian border.

Joel and I became close friends and I've always enjoyed his visits to Cincinnati and La Jolla. Whenever I am in New York, we spend time together, frequently joined for jaunts by our children. Noah, a hyperactive brat as a child, is now a tall, poised and brilliant teenager, whose company I relished in the summer of 1993 in Vermont, when my granddaughter Leila and I dropped in on the Fishers.

It was Joel who gave me the "toilet paper" collection in a fit of foolish generosity. Of course, I've added to the core holdings over the years, but he was my inspiration and has continued to mail me new specimens, filched during his travels. While he received the Orton monthly stipend, he sent me many wonderful works on paper—most of which I gave away—and one great small abstract figure in bronze (*Worls*, 1983–84; 11½" × 15" × 16"), which sits on a pedestal in my dining room.

In 1985, my friend wanted to strike his first large bronze, a compelling image inspired by the stooping form of a Buddhist monk, replete with a "cloth hump" on his back. Joel meant it to partially repay me for past kindnesses, so I agreed to underwrite the casting at a foundry. The cost far exceeded the original estimate and led to the only verbal altercation in our long association. In retrospect, I see now how naïve I was about the cost of outdoor sculpture, as it was my first experience and I lacked a proper perspective, but we resolved our differences amicably, with me agreeing to fund the production of two additional replicas from which he could derive a handsome profit. (One was sold to the eminent collector Vera List, the other to an unknown buyer.)

Originally I had intended for the work to be installed in Cincinnati, but just at that time I bought my current home in La Jolla and found the perfect spot: a grass triangle between the swimming pool and outer hedge.

Joel came to California expressly to help install the piece and he agreed readily to the spot I had selected. One day, with the help of a couple of moonlighting La Jolla Museum guards, we wrestled the five-foot, 600-pound monster into place (*The Wanderer*, 1986). As we

196

viewed our handiwork, we all shook our heads and agreed it didn't look quite right. As we mulled over the problem, one of the guards commented, "I think if it sat on a raised mound, it would look infinitely better!"

So much for *our* refined curatorial skills: The fellow was absolutely right. We headed for a building supply yard and came home with a load of cinder blocks, which became a platform, topped by a square brown marble slab. We sodded the sides with grass that blended neatly into the lawn, and on top of it all triumphantly rested *The Wanderer*, perfectly situated in a splendid setting.

Meanwhile, Joel had a series of exhibits in Europe, all well regarded. He liked being on the continent and it gave him a great excuse for extended journeys. In 1989 the Brooklyn Museum included Joel in a major show entitled "Four Americans: Aspects of Current American Sculpture" (February 24–May 15). My wife, daughter Nicole and I attended the opening and, to our minds, Joel was the star of the show. The museum had allotted him a lot of space, and most prominent of all the works displayed was a large sculpture based on *Worls* that I had at home. Joel always adored that shape and unnecessarily asked my permission to cast the large, similar edition (*Wave*, 1988; 61½″ × 78½″ × 70″). Our daughter Nicole liked it especially well, since it provided a voluminous "lap" into which she crawled, to the infinite pleasure of Joel and to the *horror* of the guards. They shouldn't have worried because it was a sturdy bronze weighing some 1,600 pounds!

Two years elapsed, and one day I had a phone call from Joel. He had heard ominous rumblings about the possible closing of Diane Brown's gallery and, presciently, he wanted to remove his large inventory from her possession prior to the collapse. *Wave* remained unsold and presented a formidable problem because of its size and weight. If I could see fit to purchase it at his cost (a considerable sum), he suggested I might direct it to some museum and eventually donate it. He assured me that a future appraisal would be high enough to prevent any financial loss, since his recent sales had all been at good prices.

Of course, I obliged Joel and arranged to ship it to the Contemporary Art Center in Cincinnati. The director, Dennis Barrie, was delighted and could visualize it being placed in the atrium of their building.

No sooner had it arrived than Dennis was peremptorily dismissed and *Wave* languished on the museum loading dock while the staff wrangled with the building owners, who saw it as an object that would block pedestrian traffic. After several months of fruitless negotiations, I decided to retain the work myself and had it shipped to La Jolla. It might be a bit large for my garden, I reasoned, but after all, Nicole would be able to climb around on it with her playmates. (An important criterion in buying garden sculpture is Nicole's reaction: She loves mounting Joel's *The Wanderer* and riding it like a horse.) Actually, *Wave* looks great at a corner of my driveway, situated on a brick foundation.

Alice Aycock

I've known Alice Aycock since 1979; after buying the *Queen's Complex*, I visited the studio loft where she dwelt and found an incredible, wide-ranging library. We forged our friendship by trading favorite titles and I left with an armful of books. Certainly, she is one of the most erudite people I've ever known, and her art is derived greatly from esoteric and common architectural forms of the past.

That year I had the brilliant idea of commissioning various artists to produce sculptures for the parks of

Cincinnati. Until then the only "art" there consisted of heroic statues of warriors or Civil War cannons. I knew the three park commissioners quite well; they were all Ivy League attorneys and each encouraged me to proceed. My grand plan was to have art students at the University of Cincinnati (where I taught) construct the major works, under the guidance of their professors. Everyone would have a fabulous learning experience, working with prominent sculptors, and the cost would be nominal, since the school had fine facilities and shops.

I approached Ellsworth Kelly, Sol LeWitt, and Alice Aycock—all cautiously receptive to my suggestion. Sol had had a bad experience in Albany, New York, where he had been pilloried for a proposal, although he was sponsored by Governor Nelson Rockefeller. So I found him badly burnt and wary, but I assured all three that I had the Park Board "in my hip pocket."

Alice was the first to face the firing line. After prodigious labor, she produced a maquette which contained a series of vertical doors erected at odd angles, in front of which was a shallow four-inch reflecting pool. It was a real winner! But all that the Harvard and Yale lawyers on the board could see were potential lawsuits. What

200

if someone drowned in the pool (a newborn baby couldn't have)? What if someone sued because of a rape behind one of the doors? Not too familiar with tort law, I listened in amazement at the exposure to litigation that the legal eagles bandied about, as they cited case histories.

Needless to say, Alice's piece was rejected and later Kelly and LeWitt fared no better (stories too long and sordid to tell). Yet one good thing came out of all this: Alice received an important commission from the Contemporary Art Center to construct a massive sculptural element under a high dome in the central gallery. This proved to be a huge artistic success, and while she was in town on the project, she stayed at my house and I had the pleasure of her company. In those years we became better acquainted, and I would see her in New York between her various tempestuous loves and marriages.

Years went by with desultory contact, until she informed me one day that she was coming to La Jolla to discuss a potential project for the Stuart Collection at UCSD; I told her it was a fortuitous coincidence, since I had been meaning to contact her about building something for the garden of my newly purchased home.

201

Alice loved my new place and chose an enclosed glen, roughly 75 by 100 feet, on a terrace below the house, which contained a miniature golf putting green, with hideous green astro-turf that I couldn't wait to remove. (The former owner was a great games player. In the lower garden was a huge croquet court with the same green covering, a shuffleboard and horseshoe area, all of which were plowed under in the name of ART.) Alice saw many possibilities and wanted to go home and think it over before coming up with a precise proposal, but we discussed certain parameters, such as budgetary considerations, which presented no real problem for her.

Alice is a dear person and usually quite lively—a pretty reddish blond who must have discovered the fountain of youth, because in her forties she looks much like the teenager she appeared to be in her twenties. Alice is also one of the most *disorganized* people I have ever known and always has led a hectic, chaotic life, lurching from one crisis to another. In her defense, part of it is *not* of her own making: Besides heading the sculpture department at Yale, commuting from New York weekly, she has the responsibility of her son, Zipper. She has had to travel around the world for the construction of her projects, or else prepare new proposals for public art. With all this has come fame: Alice is established in the firmament of art history and is very much in demand all the time.

Obviously this profile does not portray someone used to timetables or precise planning, so about two years passed before I could pin Alice down to come up with something concrete. When I finally did gain her attention, she came up with a schematic drawing that was truly spectacular. Her inspiration was the Alhambra in Granada, Spain, and she adopted several Moorish designs, repeated effectively throughout the sculpture.

Two large, interconnected concrete elements comprised the work: From the biggest one water cascades down on all sides of a raised platform, with the main stream falling over an intricate front grid into a large, rectangular basin. The fluid then courses through channels alongside the piece and ends up flowing throughout the rear structure. In addition, there is a Moorish sculptural metal element atop the main structure, four pointed oval planters containing ferns on each "corner," and surrounding the base of the entire undulating structures are inverted cast-concrete conch shells.

203

To bring this ambitious project to fruition, Alice entrusted the engineering and execution to her trusted assistant, Larry King, who came from New York and resided with us for almost seven months. My insistence that the sculpture be constructed so that it could be moved some day to a museum site added many complications that would not have arisen if the concrete had been poured on location in a single operation. Instead, many wooden molds had to be built in the lower garden (where the croquet court had been plowed under). After the numerous sections had been formed, they were lugged to the site and cemented together.

Larry employed seven graduate students from the UCSD art department as helpers (at $10 per hour) who seemed to work diligently at a snail's pace during the April–October period. What Alice had budgeted as a $30,000, six-week job extended on and on and eventually cost well over double the original estimate; but everyone was so nice and enthusiastic, any protest on my part would have been uncalled for.

Alice came with her son Zipper to supervise the progress for two weeks in June and arrived for another visit of the same duration in the autumn. The youngster was undisciplined and constantly craved his mother's attention. Interestingly, at four years of age, he seemed never to have sat down to a table for a meal, so I undertook the unsavory task of instructing him in the rudiments of civilized behavior as a "surrogate father." We got along rather well and he proved to be quite affectionate, if a trifle unruly. Zipper adored my daughter Nicole, an older woman of eight, and obeyed her incredibly well.

Meanwhile, Larry King proved to be a low-keyed, likable and well-mannered fellow, but having him stay in the guest house and eat most meals with us did create a strain on our hospitable instincts. It seemed that there was no end in sight. Yet we had a stroke of good fortune when he became captivated by a fey and appealing young woman who worked for him and, mercifully, he went to live with her for the final two months.

I rarely visited the building site, since it made me terribly depressed to see so little progress accomplished at roughly $100 per hour. Occasionally I'd talk to Alice, who would inform me cheerily that "things were coming along splendidly," suggesting that I "relax and enjoy the experience." Miraculously, the sculpture reached completion after many setbacks. The water system proved particularly tricky and I'm convinced that Larry improvised as he went along. The control panel for the pumps looks like the cockpit of a jet plane, and I've never attempted to understand the various levers and switches that regulate the water supply.

With incredible self-control, I managed to keep my cool until *The Islands of the Moons and Suns* was completed. When I thought the crew had been dismissed and the trash had been hauled away, to my surprise I found the seven students *still* working away in the lower garden: They were *removing nails from the scrap lumber!* It seemed that their professor could utilize the material, if free of metal, and they were willing to oblige. At that final indignity all the pent-up frustration derived from squandered months burst forth. I yelled and screamed at a startled Larry King, stating that I could buy a load of *new* lumber that would be far cheaper if I wished to shower largess on an unknown academician. Never before having heard me raise my voice, he cowered and admitted to a certain lapse in judgment. I regained my equanimity immediately and accepted the apology.

After completion, the entire area was relandscaped, with a low brick edging around the area and a narrow strip of grass surrounding the sculpture. On the hillside above we built a long brick viewing bench and platform, from which six people could sit and contemplate the creation.

A week later we had a gala debut party for *The Islands of the Moons and Suns* with many of the West Coast art world attending. Alice Aycock provided a guest list and we added a few personal friends. For the first time in my life, I hired caterers who proved their mettle. Since the party was devised to honor the sculptress, I was pleased to find her highly gratified at the reception and she glowed with pleasure at the universal compliments of her masterpiece. I know she considered it an important breakthrough in her art and it has spawned other "water" pieces.

Almost five years later, I report ruefully that the commissioned work has not been trouble-free. The intricate system of valves and pumps has failed on occasion and the maintenance cost has been considerable. I have no regrets. My guests and I continue to enjoy the results of Alice Aycock's genius.

Sundry Interim Acquisitions

Although half the pieces in my garden were already in existence, purchased from dealers or artists, site preparation always caused complications, and nothing was ever simple. The rest of the works were fabricated for a specific location and of course presented infinitely more complex logistical problems.

During the early years prior to *The Islands of the Moons and Suns*, a number of opportunities arose for felicitous choices.

Gene Highstein

For several years, the La Jolla Museum had three works by Gene Highstein prominently displayed on the wide concrete expanse in front of the building. Since the museum needed the space for other purposes, I received a call from Hugh Davies, the director, beseeching me to buy them for our garden. He hated to see them leave the community and perhaps saw my place as a convenient outside warehouse until he could retrieve them at a later date. They were rather compact in size and our daughter Nicole always liked crawling or leaping over them so much that she would never enter the museum proper, so, of course, I had to buy them. The sale was arranged by Highstein's dealer, the able Michael Klein, a most persuasive salesman.

All three had the same deep brown color; one resembled a small mound (15″ × 36″), a second looked like a fat bratwurst with rounded ends (18″ × 34″), and the third had the shape of a short, swollen stupa (28″ × 19″). One prominent art critic wrote rapturously about their "pure, organic forms," while a cynical, uncultured friend alluded to them as "elephant droppings."

A brick expanse in the swimming pool area presented the ideal spot to place the trio, with each separated by a discreet distance. When I requested the museum to deliver those unobtrusive, compact objects, for the first time I learned that each one, made of solid cast iron, weighed 3,000 pounds! No cadre of brawny Atlases could possibly lift and carry them to the chosen location and I wanted them exactly in the middle of my property, which had no ready access.

Certainly, if I had known in advance that I'd be responsible for carting and installing four and a half tons, I would have ignored the allure of "three Gene Highsteins" but, ever resourceful, I saw a simple answer to the problem: My neighbor's driveway ran parallel to my property beyond the towering Eugenia hedge, so it could provide a means of access. I broached the subject to the owner, explaining what would be entailed and he agreed graciously, warning me ominously that I would have to be responsible for any damage to his macadam surface.

Noting that his lane sorely needed resurfacing, as it was laced with cracks and potholes, I methodically documented the entire area with Polaroid camera shots, which would demonstrate the condition of his driveway prior to "Operation Highstein." Such foresight would eliminate future arguments with a typically precise and humorless accountant.

Moving day went like clockwork. A large crane, forklift and flatbed truck were all we needed to accomplish the job. After flawless loading at the museum, the crane deposited the forklift beside the sculptures on the truck and the convoy proceed to the adjacent driveway. Then the crane off-loaded the forklift over the hedge onto my brick walkway and, one by one, the works of art were driven around my swimming pool to the chosen site and dumped rather crudely in place (I had no worry about possible damage: They were indestructible). The expense of all this will remain locked in my breast forever, but I counsel new collectors not to be faint of heart nor worry about such trivia as *money*.

(Think always of J. P. Morgan's often cited dictum, "If you have to ask, don't have one!")

At completion, I was mightily pleased and Nicole was *ecstatic* at such a variety of challenging jumps. But my euphoria was short-lived, for I received a telephone call from the neighbor, requesting me to inspect with him the vast havoc I had caused. It did perplex me since, miraculously, there had been no fresh damage that I could spot.

Armed with my detailed photographs, hidden in my pockets, I joined him at the driveway, where he pointed out the harm I had caused from bringing in the heavy equipment. After he stopped spluttering, I coolly pulled out the evidence and methodically showed him no additional cracks or holes. At that he replied disdainfully: "These shots must have been taken *after* delivery of the art, since most of the cracks are new." Finally he admitted that the stretch had not been in mint condition and we shared the resurfacing.

Russell Sharon

I became acquainted with Hal Bromm, whose gallery showed a number of fine artists. He created a supportive environment and many of them became friends with each other. Through his introduction, my wife and I met Rosemarie Castoro, a great sculptress, and became personal friends. She has visited us in La Jolla and we see each other in New York. Some time ago I acquired a wonderful work, *Wotan* (father of the Norse gods), made of stainless steel sheet metal, now placed on our balcony.

Rosemarie, in turn, was close to Russell Sharon, another wonderful artist showing with Bromm. Russell is one of the dearest, kindest men I've ever known, so it was a privilege to get to know him as well. Rosemarie, lively and vivacious, and Russell, calm and serene, have one salient characteristic in common: They both have restless eyes and hands that ceaselessly record the magical world about them.

Rosemarie is a passionate opera buff who loves to sit in the darkened performance hall with a stack of four-by-five-inch cards on her lap, jotting down the images that dance before her eyes. These enchanting books and drawings capture the essence of that incredible amalgam of song, orchestra, dance and pageant better than written words could possibly portray. Meanwhile, Russell is incessantly filling HIS notepads with the al-

212

most childlike fancies that strike his retina. Rosemarie draws primarily with black marker; Russell usually uses watercolors or oil pastels.

When Russell visited La Jolla to choose a site for a sculpture, he spent hours daily recording his impressions of our garden as he moved quietly from one location to another. He presented our daughter Nicole with a watercolor depicting our giant Koi swimming languidly in our pond beneath a waterfall, which miraculously captured all their grace. It may be her most treasured possession.

On his first sojourn with us, he spent a leisurely week, weighing options for a project and a suitable setting. Finally, he decided that the most suitable sculptures had already been made and were currently being shown at a museum in Florida. We examined transparencies and narrowed down the choice to two: a tall, stately bird about twelve feet high and a menacing, skeletal lizard extending almost fourteen feet along the ground. Each was constructed with wooden slats that had acrylic coating in strong blues, greens or yellows.

Choosing between them was impossible, so I decided to have them both. I could envision them placed on the steep hillside above our driveway, with "Bill" the bird being chased by "Liz" the lizard, who would never quite make the capture. Russell approved my idea enthusiastically and returned a few months later to assemble the works and install them on the slope. It took quite a crew and a dazzling feat of engineering, but they have been firmly anchored to the ground and are stabilized by hidden guide wires. After more than six years they haven't budged an inch.

Russell made an agreement with me that he would provide a lifetime guarantee to keep the colors fresh and pristine (we neglected to stipulate *whose* lifetime—I am twenty-five years his senior). After a few years the colors did fade and that called for a pleasant renewal of our friendship when he came to apply a fresh coat of paint. Unfortunately, "Liz" and "Bill" seem to be holding up rather well, so I'll have to find a pretext to bring him back for another enjoyable visit. Seeing him occasionally in New York does not fulfill my need to spend time with such a wonderful friend.

Anne and Patrick Poirier

On a visit to the Sonnabend Gallery one day, Antonio Homem showed me a work he felt well suited for my garden. The artists were a Parisian couple, Anne and

Patrick Poirier. That year they were the sculptors featured at Storm King Sculpture Garden (Alice Aycock won the honor the following year). They had studied at the American Academy at Rome and became fascinated by Greco-Roman ruins, which were obsessively embodied in their later oeuvres. While not too well known in the United States, they do have a major installation in Bethesda, Maryland.

At the gallery I viewed an enchanting bird bath: Made of cast bronze, it is three feet square and contains three inches of water within the edging. Submerged within the sculpture are numerous "ruins" displaying pediments, walls and fallen columns—not dissimilar to a view of the Roman Forum, as seen from the back of the Campidoglio. To the rear is the fragment of a face, with an all-seeing eye staring blankly outward. It reaches only fifteen inches high but still towers above the scene in an omniscient way. Behind that element is a loose, heavy cast bronze sword that lies enigmatically in the trough behind the "head." Might it symbolize "Live by the sword, die by the sword"?

The details are incredible and some master craftsman spent untold hours burnishing and polishing the individual components after the original bronze casting. The patina is dark, as though the work had been excavated after centuries of entombment.

I had this installed outside my daughter's bedroom, not far from the Highstein sculptures. A bricklayer constructed a platform 30″ × 36″, thereby providing a suitable pedestal for showing the work to good advantage. The only disappointing part of the project was that birds have steered clear of it since our two cats discovered it as a drinking fountain.

Viola Frey

On my visits to New York, I usually stop by the Nancy Hoffman Gallery, where Andy Spence's wife, Sique, is the director (as well as my close friend). Normally we have a pleasant gossip and fix a dinner date during my stay. Then we tour the rooms and examine the current offerings; occasionally I have purchased the odd piece, but normally they cater to a different clientele and there is nothing of great interest to me.

However, on one visit I came upon "Fred" in a small room. (I instantly name most of my sculptures.) He was a giant, some ten feet in height, and was lying nude on his side, displaying a large penis in a state of mild excitement. Viola Frey works in ceramics and invariably uses primary colors to create startling effects.

Sique explained that "Fred" had been kept in a warehouse for several years and they had just installed him with hopes for a sale. At that, I could feel "Fred" *pleading* with me to purchase him so he could return to California, the place of his birth. He hated the Big Apple and wanted to be back in the Golden State; I freed him from enslavement and arranged to have him shipped to La Jolla.

My first thought was to place "Fred" in the bottom of our swimming pool at the deep end, but, plaintively, Nicole mentioned that she liked to dive and he would displace an enormous amount of space. So I relented and he is now reposing serenely a few feet from the edge of the pool under a cluster of palm fronds.

Ann Preston

Not long afterwards I stopped by Barbara Toll Gallery, near our loft on Greene Street. At the time Barbara represented Andy Spence and also was a member of an informal support group of women who owned galleries, which included Annie Plumb and Nancy Hoffman. (I think they gained strength through their loose affiliation with each other.)

Barbara was showing the work of Ann Preston, a sculptress who teaches at Cal-Arts in Valencia, California, and who has a solid reputation and does splendid work. The centerpiece of the exhibit, in the middle of the front room, was a "fountain" that had become famous throughout Soho for its uniqueness. I had heard adjectives ranging from "disgusting" to "ingenious," and Ann had achieved fame, if not notoriety, so I had to see firsthand what had triggered such vehement comments.

A concrete receptacle, seven feet in diameter and nine inches high, contained in its center a platform, at the same height, on which sat a fascinating bronze sculpture. The space between the outer circular wall and the inner pedestal held a pool of water.

The sculpture consisted of two graceful, nubile, androgynous figures—both obviously contortionists—facing each other and bent over so far that their heads were between their legs, with mouths upturned, while each pair of hands held a copper "glass." With an ingenious series of concealed copper tubes and pumps, water dropped into the cups, which overflowed to the

218

gaping mouths and, eventually, poured out of their anuses in an arcing stream into the pool below.

It presented an unusual effect, and the very fact that it seemed to shock so many people provided a strong incentive for me to own the work.

So Barbara shipped me "Castor and Pollux" (for lack of a better name) and, after some months, the artist arrived to put the disassembled pieces together. Ann Preston is a bubbling, delightful person, and it was a treat to get to know her. She knew her engineering rather well, but it was far from simple to prepare the site and put all elements in working order. We placed it on a small grass strip—almost beside the tennis court, where there was ready access to both power and water—so, with the help of a plumber, electrician, and brawny gardeners, C and P were installed successfully.

It is quite a conversation piece and usually gives rise to rather ribald remarks from guests; one gynecologist pointed out that it was anatomically *incorrect*, which seemed to distress him. Actually, the two figures suffer from periodic bouts of "vomiting" and "diarrhea," causing frequent visits by the indefatigable "Pond Doctor," who has to fine-tune their inner organs. Leaves and detritus have a way of constantly clogging the crucial filtering system, so proper maintenance is a never-ending ordeal. All that notwithstanding, I have only warm feelings toward Ann's creation.

I have noted a certain disdain from the art establishment's professional denizens toward my feeble attempts to combine humor with art. "Fred," "Bill" and "Liz"—as well as "Castor and Pollux"—tend to provoke derisive sneers, while curators and directors have rapturous orgasms over Highstein's amorphous forms. Their preciosity leaves me flabbergasted.

Giuseppe Penone

Giuseppe Penone, a sculptor from Turin, Italy, is little known in the U.S., although he has a noted reputation in Europe. He is represented by Marian Goodman in New York, who brought him to my attention. Since he skillfully combines elements of culture and nature (a dominant theme in my garden), I was immediately attracted to his body of work.

Since Marian had no examples of Penone's work in America, we perused the catalogue of a recent European show and selected one of his very impressive works that was for sale. Still incredibly naïve, I failed to check the exact size and weight of the bronze, or the methodology for installation.

One fine day a huge wooden crate arrived by air freight, which the local trucker deposited unceremoniously just inside the gate of the lower garden. Removing the top, we found a seven-foot human figure that weighed 600 pounds, but we lacked any instructions regarding how to erect the piece.

A close examination of the Turin Gallery photograph in the brochure revealed a line of twelve large clay pots, each containing plantings. Balanced on the rims of the last two were the feet of the massive male abstraction, a precarious feat at best. We had no clue as to how this miracle had been achieved, since clay pots are low-fired and fragile, susceptible to crumbling under such enormous weight. I therefore appealed to Marian to obtain detailed instructions from the artist on how to proceed.

Months passed without a word as "Charlie"—which I dubbed the bronze—languished in his open pine coffin. Frustrated, I then resorted to faxing Penone with a plaintive cry for assistance, ultimately receiving a crude sketch from him that added nothing to what we already knew. Finally, in desperation, I enlisted the help of Ben

Anderson, Italo Scanga's artist son-in-law, who came up with an innovative solution.

The site I had chosen was in a corner of the lower garden, adjacent to a cluster of bamboo shoots which extended over forty feet high. The artist had instructed that bamboo be planted in the last pot so that it would grow through the arms of the bronze figure—and I liked the idea of echoing the bamboo motif.

The male bronze is represented by a fragmentary shell that deftly outlines a human—as much by negative space as by the metal itself. Legs and feet are firmly implanted and one arm is curved and outstretched, as though holding an enormous fluffy pillow. The other arm lies close to the body, and metal twigs simulate fingers. The "head" is a featureless face, which flows from the hollow torso.

Anderson's creative answer was to place two strong metal rods in a wide and deep bed of concrete. Then he drilled holes in the bottom of two fourteen-inch pots, which he placed over the rods. Finally, with the help of a crew, he welded the rods to "Charlie's" feet. Afterwards we planted bamboo in the first pot, a wide-leafed shrub in the second, followed by five containing Cotoneaster plants with bright red berries, and the last five

222

with a different narrow-leaf green shrub. All twelve containers bisect the corner at forty-five degrees, with "Charlie" perfectly "balanced" on the first two pot rims. What a tour de force! A few discerning people have divined the trick, but usually we receive lavish compliments about such an incredible installation.

One of my many curatorial duties has been to train the bamboo to grow through "Charlie's" outstretched arm, and in five years I've made considerable progress, after a few false starts and replantings. Today the shoots have taken root firmly and have established a strong symbiosis with their host.

Italo Scanga

My friend Italo deserves a chapter, if not an entire book. Our lives have been intertwined for some fifteen years (and by now he is close to my children and grandchildren, as I am to his numerous offspring). Italo, born in an obscure village tucked away in Calabrian mountains, came to the United States as a boy and received a superior education. I consider him to be one of the most erudite men I know, although he would probably protest that depiction. His wide-ranging knowledge of history, fine arts, music, philosophy and poetry never fails

223

to astound me. Our encounters, however, are infrequent, since he travels a lot to exhibitions of his work; also, he is much in demand as panelist and lecturer and, being a workaholic, more often than not he is buried in his studio—if not teaching at UCSD, where he is a prestigious, tenured full professor.

Italo, Latin to the core, with a volatile temperament, proudly betrays his peasant background. (He regularly visits his native soil to see his many relatives.) He speaks English fluently, Italian abominably and is at his best in "Calabrese." But he is never at a loss for words in *any* language, as he flaunts his biased opinions indiscriminately.

Under Italo's rather gruff exterior lurks the proverbial heart of gold. He is a warm-hearted, generous-spirited man who has spent his life helping others. In the back-biting art world he is notable for the constant support he has afforded struggling artists to launch embryonic careers. Indeed, many stars attribute their success to his mentoring and often come to pay homage. It always amazes me how Italo seems to know everyone in the art world—and rarely in a superficial way. By now the name Italo Scanga is well recognized throughout the world.

At the same time Italo is not devoid of prejudices, which come pouring forth at the slightest provocation. He loves well and hates with the same intensity. At times I have appalled him by purchasing the work of an artist he despises; he feels a betrayal on my part for having made an odious selection. Often he sighs resignedly, with a shrug of the shoulder, only to return to the subject at a later date, chiding me on my lack of discrimination. Yet, on the whole, he has been supportive of my efforts.

Italo Scanga personifies the public's image of an artist. He dresses scruffily, often sporting a jaunty beret. His studio could be the set for *La Bohème*, containing an indescribable clutter of objects that he acquires weekly at the local stadium swap meet. Much of this flotsam finds itself eventually embedded into his sculptures, which he produces in awesome numbers. The studio itself is a work of art, crammed with his framed paintings on paper and glass pieces blown in Seattle at the studio of his best friend, Dale Chihuly. Finished sculptures, mountains of books, catalogues, religious objects and the culls of the swap meet all present a mind-boggling sight.

When I first moved to La Jolla, I came armed with an

introduction provided by our mutual friend, Scott Burton—but a year elapsed before I made the effort to meet Italo. At that time he had a small show in La Jolla at the Thomas Babeor Gallery, which I visited with my house guest, Daniel Weinberg, a San Francisco dealer. We were both intrigued by what we saw, so I telephoned Italo the next day and arranged a studio visit. Back then he had quarters in an old water tower on the UCSD campus, which had been divided into working space for faculty members of the art department.

Weinberg and I were overwhelmed by the vast quantity of wonderful art that greeted us. Every nook and cranny, as well as a large balcony above, was so crowded that one scarcely knew where to step. (We later learned that this was just the tip of the iceberg, and that his home and garage were also crammed with completed works.) On the spot, Daniel decided to give Italo a show and they spent several days sifting through various options in preparation for the exhibit. The prices were so reasonable that Daniel decided to buy the work outright for cash, much to the sculptor's delight. I stepped aside until their transactions were completed before making my purchases, but Daniel graciously bowed to my wishes in several instances.

In the late seventies, minimal and conceptual art were all the rage and Italo was decidedly not in the mainstream. Uncompromisingly, he continued to march to his own drummer and, as a result, his sales had dwindled to near zero. Colorful, fanciful art—as well as religious themes—were OUT and he didn't stand a chance. During the ensuing two years, except for Daniel Weinberg, I believe I was his only buyer, but during that period I bought a *lot* of his art!

It upset me that trendsetters could so narrowly define art, so I was determined to assist him as our friendship ripened. I embarked on a campaign to introduce his art through gifts to prominent museums, and achieved a measure of success in the years that followed. Chicago, Philadelphia, Cincinnati and the Guggenheim all received major works, and Berkeley got a wonderful "Potato Famine" piece (one of a great series). The director, Jim Elliott, violated strict guidelines which forbade the display of any art by the staff of the University of California system—but wisely broke the rule, since the sculpture was very exceptional.

Meanwhile, my home became crowded with Italo's work. Each time I visited his studio or home, I made new acquisitions. Some years earlier he had started

227

painting simple, charming drawings on the backs of tin can wrappers. One would be the label from a tomato can, another a narrow strip from a tuna fish can. They proved irresistible, so I bought slews of them to give away to family and friends. During the same period, he made delectable small paintings on shaped metal sheets, all tastefully matted and framed in natural dark woods, which I also bought.

For Italo, nothing is simple: The more complex a deal, the better he likes it. Perhaps it stems from the collective unconscious of his conniving peasant ancestors. Barter has enormous appeal to his fertile mind. One day he invited me to his studio to peruse his latest output. Before my eyes were four enormous heads, made of wood in cubistic style, each over three feet high. They were the latest in a series of heads in various sizes that I had inadvertently inspired a couple of years before.

As I stood admiring his prodigious efforts, he suggested coyly that perhaps I might like one in exchange for my old but sturdy Volvo sedan, which he had been coveting for some time. I found him irresistible and burst out laughing. After negotiations too abstruse to repeat, the transaction was completed to his satisfaction. The "head" ended up at the Chicago Art Institute.

After lunch one day at his studio, he had me pose for a few minutes while he drew my profile on the back of a soiled envelope. Some days later he presented me with a sculpture of my head and shoulders, which bore absolutely no resemblance to the subject. I then commissioned him to do one of Inga, my companion of the moment. Somehow, this time he captured her beautiful Swedish essence very well. I gave "Inga" to the La Jolla Museum.

Those heads started Italo on a road to great financial bounty. The first two were monochromatic and simply delineated. Soon he was producing cubistic heads, with a variety of colors painted on the various planes and before long I was swamped in heads—small, medium-sized and large—before they began selling like hot cakes to collectors. The "Chicago" acquisition was the ultimate purchase I made of that series.

Along with the "Potato Famine" series, I think back on Italo's monochromatic "Fear" series as being my all-time favorites. Of sixteen major works in that group, I acquired six—almost all in 1980: *Fear of Self*, *Fear of*

War, *Fear of Flying* and *Woman on Fire*, I recall most distinctly. I am sorry to report that I don't own any of them now.

One day Italo invited me to his studio for lunch (an almost sure-fire signal that he had something diabolical in the offing). Before long he revealed that he needed $3,000 so he could take a trip to Italy. In exchange, he suggested providing me with a selection of art from his studio. What would I like? After agreeing to the proposition, I wandered about the area—which was, as usual, knee-deep in art—pointing out those items I thought especially attractive: "Italo, that one's a honey and that over there is especially good." I continued noting objects of my affection, which were quite numerous. Italo finally stopped me, saying, "I've got the idea," and I wrote him a cheque for $3,000.

A few days later, his assistant arrived at my home in a pickup truck which was overflowing with sculptures. I was overwhelmed by the mass of material that Italo had delivered in recompense for my advance payment. He had priced major works at a paltry few hundred dollars apiece. Italo might be a knave at heart, but he was rather an uncalculating fool when it came to his friends.

A day or so later, I called Italo, saying that I had not received an invoice for his art, which I needed in order to keep a proper inventory on my computer. He replied sweetly: "Please make up your own invoice and send me a copy of it for my records."

Not many years after we met, Italo had a rare opportunity: An exceedingly wealthy Texan, Laura Carpenter, was opening a new gallery on lower West Broadway, and she sought out artists with a solid reputation to represent exclusively. With boldness, she picked known artists a bit out of fashion—and she *sorely* wanted Italo in her stable.

Italo chose me to be his consultant during negotiations, and I deemed it politic to remain the anonymous Svengali behind the scenes. Their meetings were long and arduous, but she inadvertently displayed her eagerness, so I had him hold out for most favorable terms. In the end, she guaranteed Italo a minimum of $100,000 over a three-year period, no matter what sales might be forthcoming. Generously, she started buying his works outright in contemplation of the first show. By this time, with my coaching, Italo had raised prices considerably, but they were still very reasonable. He was ecstatic at the deal he had struck, for it was more money than he had ever dreamed of to supplement his university stipend.

Barely two weeks later Italo had a visit from an important collector who wished to make some purchases. When that transpired, Italo could not bring himself to report the sales to his exclusive agent, as he considered it his divine right to make direct sales to collectors. Of course, eventually Laura Carpenter got wind of what was going on and an unholy donnybrook ensued that broke up their holy alliance. Italo is not temperamentally suited to being exclusively represented by *anyone*.

On another occasion I served as Italo's consultant. He and his wife, Stephanie, were in the middle of a divorce and they had initiated a phase of endless squabbling over issues large and small. Since my wife and I were friends of both, Italo sought my counsel about future tactics. He had certainly come to the right place, since I had had plenty of *personal* divorce experience.

My advice was simple: "Italo, be generous in your settlement with Stephanie and don't quibble over trivial matters. In the long run, whatever it costs you now will seem unimportant later, since you are a successful artist with impressive earning power. Above all, avoid abrasive encounters with her for your own peace of mind." He thanked me effusively and pledged to follow the words of wisdom I had proffered.

Ten days later Stephanie came to our house for dinner. She could barely contain her distress with what Italo had just perpetrated: The previous Sunday, she had gone to her door stoop to pick up the *Los Angeles Times*, which was missing. She called the circulation department to send out another copy and they did so obligingly, however assuring her that her paper had *definitely* been delivered.

The next Sunday the *Times* was missing again, so, suspecting foul play, Stephanie telephoned Italo to see if *he* knew of the paper's whereabouts. He immediately replied: "Of course I know. It is MY paper since I paid for the subscription, so I came over to retrieve it." To accomplish that mission he had driven three miles—while, just across the street from his residence, was a Seven-Eleven where he could have easily obtained the Sunday *Times*. After that incident, I considered it appropriate to resign from my consulting role.

Italo's "swapping" instincts remain unrequited. When he comes to my house, he always paces around, examining objects with an enquiring eye, as though he is constantly reassessing my cultural taste. One evening

233

he announced it unfair that I had *three* LeWitt drawings stashed away unseen on my sitting room balcony,
while he had none. At that he tucked one of them under
his arm and stated that the next time I visited his studio
he'd give me plenty of art to make up for his flagrant
theft. I couldn't take my friend to task and later he gave
me two splendid "heads" that I bestowed on my children Eddie and Robin.

As my sculpture garden evolved, Italo pointed out
that I had nothing of his (the house, though, is full of
his work). When I replied that he had never offered me
anything suitable, he invited me to a large field at the
university, stacked with forty-foot sea containers, in
which UCSD professors stored their surplus art. With
flashlight in hand, we crept into one of his containers
and rummaged about to find some large ceramic heads
that he had produced one summer at a Midwest college. Italo is always full of surprises and there, in that
container, I viewed six superb cubistic works. Finally, I
chose a favorite to put in the garden, where it sits on a
well-designed cedar stand. White and light blue, the
face stares out benevolently from a small glade, surrounded by camellia bushes.

One of my prized possessions, which hangs in my

office above the computer desk, is a large black-and-white Conti crayon drawing by Italo of our beloved friend, Scott Burton. Drawn in 1986, it predated the onslaught of AIDS, although we knew Scott's health was declining rapidly even then. It serves as a constant reminder of a special genius and of the others who have suffered a similar fate. Somehow it seems to encapsulate not only a great artistic talent, but also a sensitive soul.

Dan Graham

Dan Graham is lauded as an original thinker who has written and lectured widely, expounding his theories of art—although I find him tongue-tied and monosyllabic. In all honesty, I have never been sure just *what* he has said, although he claims I am an empathic conversationalist who really understands him.

Marian Goodman, who represents him, insisted that I had to have a "Dan Graham," and she proved correct. Without doubt it is the most successful work in my garden, although I find it difficult to analyze why. Dan has had recurring bouts of ill health, which caused a long delay before his first visit. Even after he picked a spot on the grass of our lower garden, it took several years for him to make a specific proposal. His missing exact dimensions entailed yet further delays.

Concurrently, I had contacted artist Michael Singer and, between the two of them, it seemed like a race between tortoise and snail. They ended up in a near tie, although Dan's project got finished first.

When I finally did capture Dan's attention, he proved reasonably diligent, taking endless pains with the smallest details. I employed David Jurist, then a graduate student taking a degree in landscape architecture, to bring the "sculpture" to fruition, and he followed the artist's instructions. (Sometimes when he needed guidance, the work stopped for months until David could chase down the artist in New York or Germany, where Dan resided much of the time.)

The piece is simplicity itself, yet difficult to describe, since its effect is so subtle. Graham considers it a "maze," although certainly not in any literal sense. The basic elements are two-way mirrors and hedges that produce an incredible optical illusion. Facing a viewer on the lawn to the left is a privet hedge, eight feet square, framed by four-inch gray metal strips. At ninety degrees to the right-hand edge is a two-way mirror of the same dimension. At ninety degrees to the rear of the mirror is another eight-foot-square unframed hedge (parallel to the first one, but eight feet back). Finally, a second identical mirror faces along the same plane; on the left of its frame is a three-foot mirror at ninety degrees toward the rear attached to it. To the right of the second eight-foot mirror at ninety degrees is *another* hedge of identical size (exactly parallel to the first mirror).

As one regards the work, the maze appears, since the hedges and mirrors interplay to create the illusion of considerable depth and, as one walks around the construct, images shift constantly due to the changing reflections. The dominant word that comes to mind is SERENITY. Great beauty has been created with the plainest materials and the most incredibly intelligent design!

Today the Dan Graham work is in stable condition. The gardener washes the glass panes and trims the greenery on a regular schedule—but to arrive at this felicitous moment took years of anguish. Commissioned sculpture does not come easily. If I ignored the difficulty in liaison with the artist—who took no responsibility for the construction—we still faced the problem of fabricating and assembling the right materials. Eight-foot two-way shatter-proof glass was not readily available, and the final supplier was slow in making it. The "simple" frames proved anything but simple, and the twelve-inch-wide cement troughs containing the plantings—while aesthetically balancing the whole piece—ended up far too narrow for eight-foot plants to flourish. I installed sprinklers to assure regular watering, which was a major headache as well.

Dan and I toured La Jolla homes, visited nurseries and consulted gardening books to find the appropriate foliage. He settled on Potacarpus—a feathery broadleaf. Filling the beds cost a fortune and they never did well. I used to visit them daily to cajole them into growth, but they wilted and died just the same. By mistake, we replanted the same genus with equally disastrous results. At the third foray, my gardener opted for English privet—a hardy species, somewhat stubborn about growing expeditiously. So, after five years, full of frustration, our "Dan Graham" (it defies a nickname) has finally reached full maturity.

Just as we reached this state of equilibrium, I received a request from Hugh Davies, director of the La Jolla

Museum: Would I please consider donating the work to *their* new sculpture garden? I replied: "The matter will be under advisement by our board of directors."

Michael Singer

One evening I fantasized in leisurely fashion about whom I would like to commission to do a garden piece. Suddenly I came up with the name: Michael Singer. Three years earlier, in 1984, I had seen his wonderful exhibit at the Guggenheim Museum, which had left an indelible impression on me.

I made enquiries in the art world about how to contact him, but came up with no helpful clue. His name evinced positive comments, but I could only glean that he was a recluse who lived *somewhere* in northern New England. Eighteen months later I found Michael via Angela Westwater, who represented him—although he rarely had a gallery show.

After an exchange of letters in March 1989, we arranged a La Jolla meeting for that June. Michael is another personification of artist: long gray tresses streaming down his neck, a small goatee below a pleasant countenance, and wearing nondescript work clothes. He seemed quite agreeable and low-keyed, but

239

I immediately sensed a major intelligence as he enunciated the basis for his art. Sensitive to environmental issues, he had branched far from being an artist creating individual works.

In recent years he had made successful proposals for major projects. To bring them to fruition, he formed and supervised teams of architects, engineers, landscape specialists, and highly skilled craftsmen. Many had studied at MIT, where Michael taught, and traveled about the United States, as well as Europe, on various assignments. His budget could run into tens of millions of dollars, as he dealt with eliminating urban blight or reclaiming tracts of desert wasteland.

Since I've known Michael, he has transformed a long stretch of riverbank into parkland in Flint, Michigan. He is now putting the finishing touches on a giant recycling center in Phoenix, which is situated in the middle of a vast park, designed with diverse amenities to attract citizens. All the sites contain spacious sculptural elements, expressly made for each specific location. At Denver Airport, Michael is in the process of installing a monster which contains his signature elements of cedar or redwood, Vermont granite and metal—more often than not bronze, cast in a secret technique to closely resemble wooden pieces.

Farleigh-Dickinson College has a large piece of his in the atrium of a building and, just recently, Wellesley College obtained one for its new art museum. Michael draws like a whiz and the works on paper are breathtakingly wonderful. In addition, he occasionally publishes private books of etchings—equally wonderful.

Michael had never had a private commission, but he liked the idea when he saw my property. Since he had commuted to Phoenix—an hour's flight away—for several years, he and his staff would be conveniently located. He quickly picked where he wanted to work: Starting at the second-floor apartment above the garage was a steep path that led up a hill, ending at a ridge, where a spectacular scene of the ocean and northern shoreline burst into view! Situated on that spot was a nondescript gazebo with a red tile roof. The long path was *far* from user-friendly. Small round stone aggregate "steps" were well embedded at regular intervals, surrounded by gravel in the vain hope of stemming erosion. Women in high heels could never navigate the incline. A final drawback was the barren expanse to the

241

right of the path. Under the shade of four fig, apricot and nectarine trees, ground cover just never grew, leaving a bald, unattractive eyesore.

Michael could immediately visualize what he wanted to achieve. He would redesign the entire area with new hillside ground cover, a new path and gazebo, as well as two sculptural pieces along the rise to the right, culminating in a large one at the summit. I had difficulty in understanding precisely what he saw so clearly in his mind's eye, but he promised to supply detailed drawings and a final maquette. Most encouraging was his promised precise planning. Once our budget had been set, the project would be at a fixed fee, with some flexibility allowed for unknown contingencies. He guaranteed performance in timely fashion, after scoffing at the "unprofessional" conduct of Alice Aycock, who made me suffer so long with a substantial cost overrun and tardiness that ran into months.

At the outset, Michael and I agreed that there would be, in essence, two intertwined but separate projects. The first entailed the improvement of the landscaping and construction of a new gazebo. Quite separately, there would be the sculptures themselves. They were to be designed to later find a place in a museum or public park.

One month after Michael's visit, I first met Sterling McMurrin, who visited the prospective site. Sterling is a fine fellow, aptly named, who studied under Michael at MIT. After obtaining his architectural degree, he cast his lot with his mentor and provided leadership in all principal projects. He liked the wide gamut of challenges in the work, which suited his personality.

Sterling did a lot of measuring after studying the land contours, and left with a wealth of information. That summer a team started the detailed planning and construction of a model; after completing this phase, Michael suggested a visit to his Shangri-la in Vermont. (Angela Westwater told me I had been given the supreme compliment. She had been there only once and almost no one was ever invited.)

On a glorious autumn day, I arrived in Wilmington, Vermont, and checked into a local inn where Michael greeting me warmly and took me for a tour of his estate. He has a charming house and numerous structures on the property, including a principal studio for constructing sculptures, barns outfitted to store and display finished work, as well as one isolated building used exclusively for drawing.

A large, topographical rendition of our project had been meticulously built and set up in the main studio. Michael, Sterling and I had our first detailed discussion about the various elements. Obviously a lot of thought had already been given, so it was now a matter of devising a precise budget to which I gave my blessing, since I was thrilled at Michael's vision.

By January 1990, I had the provisional budget, which well exceeded what we originally had in mind. Through pleasant negotiations, we decided to eliminate the two sculptural elements alongside the path and concentrate on the principal one by the gazebo, which substantially reduced the cost. Michael assented to the change. Within a month, we had a concrete plan and I sent on my first cheque so the work could begin. Everything would be made in Vermont and later trucked to La Jolla for final installation.

After various delays, work began in June and continued through the summer. In mid-September, a large covered van arrived at my home, where a vast quantity of bits and pieces were unloaded and placed on the garage apron. Sterling, his brother Joe, and two master carpenters arrived from Vermont, to be assisted by a crew of six Mexicans who worked for Luis Garcia, a local landscaping specialist.

Everyone proved to be highly competent and diligent. The language barrier presented no problem, and a group of able men seemed to enjoy working as a team. The excavation of a cavity in the hillside summit was first priority and this became a major snag. Despite a careful prior survey, the amount of dirt to be displaced far exceeded the original estimate by several-fold. The sculpture called for a massive hole to be buttressed by redwood siding as insurance against possible landslide. (As an additional precaution, the raw slopes were planted densely with ivy.) Ground preparation took far longer than anticipated. Rather than hand-carry shovelfuls of dirt down the hill, the workmen strewed the material over a large expanse of the hillside; the thin layer would be easily absorbed into the soil later on.

The rest of the work proceeded expeditiously: The old gazebo was demolished, although the foundation and floor would be utilized for the new structure. The many sculptural and gazebo elements, all carefully numbered for proper positioning, had to be hauled on strong shoulders up the steep incline as construction got under way. A cheerful, industrious cadre started early each day and toiled until dusk.

Sterling exercised exemplary leadership, and proved his mettle when crises arose that called for improvisation. Despite careful precautions (everything had been assembled completely in Vermont to check for flaws, before being taken apart for shipping), problems did arise with regularity, calling for impromptu solutions. Good-humored Al, the master carpenter, and his assistant were masters of improvisation, such as when bolts didn't fit properly or the swing couldn't be set up according to plan. They appeared never at a loss for an ingenious solution.

When all the materials had been toted to the site, the Mexicans demolished the old stepping stones and commenced regrading. Joe McMurrin took charge of that operation and began construction of the new steps leading uphill. He found preformed concrete rectangles well suited for the purpose and smaller blocks for edging on each side. Then he planted ground cover between steps—as well as on both sides—to stabilize the land. Joe must be the most painstaking, patient man in the world. He crept along on his hands and knees for days, carefully measuring with a level and T-square to ensure that *each* stone was placed exactly right. Just as diligently, he supervised the laborers, who covered the large barren area with baby tears, eminently suitable for growth in shade.

Instead of two weeks, the project took five, with Joe lingering later to finish the path. I ended up with a very special sculpture—a gazebo, sublimely beautiful and reminiscent of a simple Japanese structure—and an eminently serviceable path, quite aesthetically pleasing as well. The cost well exceeded the 8 percent contingency reserve, but I waived our agreement about a fixed price and willingly paid in full.

In the more than three years since installation, the work has taken on a life of its own, as the ground cover and ivy have flourished. It took a long while for the ivy on the hillside to take hold and cover that area. More ivy was planted in trays on the roof of the gazebo, and only now have they started hanging down as planned. An intricate watering system needs constant attention and occasional repairs (which are sometimes overlooked by my gardener). Yet the gazebo bower is becoming surrounded by shrubbery and the plantings inside apertures of the retaining wall are finally doing well (through overwatering, due to a faulty sprinkler system, they rotted out and had to be replanted once). The ground cover on the floor of the sculpture has also spread out perfectly.

By the second year, Joe's ground cover had engulfed the naked slope and presented a solid green sheen to the hillside—and the summit area had reached a certain maturity. Tragedy struck when an army of skunks who evidently love baby tears invaded our property. In a matter of days, they had torn gaping holes in our pristine surroundings.

A knowledgeable friend informed me that skunks are allergic to moth balls, so we bought out the supply at a neighborhood store and strewed the camphor throughout the area. The gambit appeared to work, so we replanted the baby tears—at no small cost. Yet before long, the skunks ignored our handiwork and again dug them up.

I ended up calling "Critter Control," a service that traps noxious animals alive and hauls them away. Too soon, I replanted, only to have the skunks return from wherever Critter Control had hauled them. Ignominiously defeated, I refused to replant.

I relished the idyllic retreat, gazing at the entrancing

248

view. Friends came to chat and share a drink atop, and Nicole plays around the area with her companions.

One day in the winter of 1993, Michael telephoned, asking permission to let the L.A. Wellesley Alumna Club come and view his handiwork in April. I agreed.

When Michael and Sterling arrived two days before the ladies, they set to work to spruce up the place. They bought many trays of baby tears from a nursery and replanted the numerous bald spots. They scrubbed the cloth cushions of the swing, trimmed the ivy around the sculpture, washed the floor of the gazebo. The place looked really scrumptious. Michael and I passed the time chatting pleasantly and I had a chance to state in person my disappointment at the outcome of the Wellesley gift, * which I had done solely to help a friend. Everything seemed amicable enough at the time.

---

*In 1991 I had donated a major work of Michael's to Wellesley College, since he sorely needed a benefactor. I paid him a large sum, based on what he claimed to obtain elsewhere; but when I received the official appraisal from the Art Dealers' Association (an organization well respected by IRS), it came to only two thirds the amount I had been told. This left me very unhappy and I looked to Michael for financial redress. He offered to compensate me with another work—an idea I rejected—and eventually gave Nicole a lovely folio, which still left me rankled. At one point he indicated that I could afford the loss better than he—in fact, he didn't have the money to pay me. I am still skeptical of that statement, as by inference he has a substantial income and more than adequate lifestyle.

The Wellesley contingent enjoyed their visit and I enjoyed having them. They proved to be a knowledgeable group, enthusiastically touring my garden, guided by Michael. Until then I didn't know that he liked the other artists' work—most artists aren't that generous of spirit. So I labeled the day a resounding success, as he seemed quite pleased at the outcome.

But I couldn't have been more wrong: Ten days later I received a two-page letter from him, reciting in polite language how upset he was at the condition of his work. In fact, if I couldn't do better in the future, he asked respectfully that I never again use his name in context with the work.

One particular grievance was well justified. Unknown to me, daughter Nicole had garlanded his bronze and stone elements with flowers plucked from below—all of which had wilted and died. Moreover, she had taken small pebbles and stones and dotted them around, purportedly creating cabalistic signs! If I had known of her desecration prior to the Singer arrival, I'd have cleaned up her act; yet there it remained, exposed to his wrath.

Other matters also deeply distressed him. The ivy

had crept over the walls and hadn't had a proper trimming. Correctly, he noted the gazebo was a bit messy through constant use and, above all, the skunks' ravages appalled him. As a footnote to his diatribe, he noted that he was enclosing a bill for the plantings. Would I please reimburse him for $358.89? That request outraged me the most and I have since completely severed relations with Michael Singer.

However, I'm pleased to add a cheerful postscript: My gardener and unofficial curator, the resourceful Ben Rivas, and I have finally devised a way to defeat the skunks. He found a light, strong nylon scrim—barely visible to the naked eye—with which we covered the enormous area, including the space around the steps. Once again we planted extensively and the baby tears grew quickly through the netting, totally concealing it, and the skunks have migrated to more receptive pastures.

Sundry Commissions

Since 1989, a number of fine artists have visited me, picked a site and fabricated sculptures in their studios. Each time the installation involved little more than minimal ground preparation and, on occasion, a quick-drying cement foundation. I purr with pleasure, thinking about how pain-free it all was—a veritable inspiration for the future.

David Teeple

In Holyoke, Massachusetts, David Teeple has a large studio where he pounds metal plates with a sledgehammer, welds bronze to steel and works in wood as well. This provides a suitable outlet for his vibrant physical energy, which reflects itself in his work. One can feel immediately his boundless power.

I met David through our mutual friend, Sarah Vogeler. At the time he lived in Arizona. Wonderfully warm and pleasant, he is quite lovable, so members of the family welcomed him eagerly on his first of many visits. Whenever he comes, we play lots of tennis and gossip about art for hours on end, as he brings me up to date on his career successes and disappointments.

He and I chose a spot alongside the towering hedge that flanks the swimming pool. The Eugenia has hues of rich green tinged with brown, which I wished to be mirrored in his piece, so he made a sculptural element, 55″×25″, from fourteen steel plates welded into a rectangle. Each plate, of varying size, has been torn and twisted through incessant battering and some have holes ripped through. All over the surface, bronze pellets have been fused, giving an appearance of many tiny fingers eerily groping downward.

Somehow David achieved a perfect patina, since the colors blend superbly with the tints from the hedge. Ingeniously, the piece is so constructed that it can be reversed "easily," as each side is quite different. In principle I have two sculptures instead of one but when I tried to switch it around with the help of a friend, the sheer weight overwhelmed us and we surrendered in complete exhaustion. I remain quite pleased with it just the way it stands.

Ellen Driscoll

In the 1980s two large buildings in Soho were renovated for accommodating art galleries; 560 and 568 Broadway face each other on the east side of the street, separated by Prince Street, and they filled up rapidly due to enticing rental rates. (Unsuspecting dealers didn't read the fine print and faced horrendous escalations after a few years elapsed.) I would wander from floor to floor, discovering a new breed of art dealer who was showing interesting young people's work at afford-able prices.

Damon Brandt was one, whom I found to be exceed-ingly gracious and very committed to the artists he rep-resented. Ellen Driscoll had an impressive show with him and I expressed immediate interest in offering her a commission. Just at that time, she received a de-servedly favorable review in the *Times* and her career rocketed from obscurity to wide recognition.

With publicity, she became quite busy, preparing sculptures for various shows as well as private collec-tors, so Ellen kept deferring a promised visit to La Jolla for a discussion about a commission. After endless de-lays and canceled dates, she finally appeared. I found her to be simple and direct, without a trace of the ar-rogance that sometimes afflicts other newly minted successes. To my surprise, I learned that her mother was headmistress of the Lotspeich School in Cincinnati, where I—and my children—had received superb ele-mentary education.

We chose a small, triangular grassy area alongside the brick wall leading to the lower garden as a site. Upon her return to New York she made a detailed drawing. It looked great to me and I gave my immediate approval. The fabrication had quite a few bottlenecks, so it was a long time before the piece finally arrived at my home.

When we finally opened the crate at the site, I gazed in horror, as the piece barely resembled what I had envisioned. Not trusting my memory, I reexamined the drawing, which was only vaguely similar. Besides certain structural changes, what I received was far *larger* than planned so it overwhelmed the narrow strip and looked exceedingly awkward there. As a temporary expedient we moved the sculpture to an adjacent wide bed of ivy that lies between the grass and the boundary fence. Fortunately, it looked quite wonderful there.

Ellen Driscoll's sculpture is roughly ten feet long and vaguely reminds me of an old-fashioned auto horn from the 1920s. At one extremity is a large "bulb" from which extends a wide, round tube that gently curves to an eventual ninety degrees, ending up attached to a "cornucopia" aperture. Entirely sheathed in thin copper plates, the color is a deep gray-brown except for the interior end of the claxon (cornucopia), which has a lovely pale blue patina.

Still in a state of shock at the variance from our orig-

255

inal plan, I contacted Damon Brandt to express my dismay. He explained that Ellen had run into technical problems that precluded fabricating the work as originally envisioned, but she hoped I'd be as pleased as she was at the final outcome. Damon then made the gentlemanly offer to take the sculpture off my hands. I couldn't hurt Ellen's feelings. She is a fine artist and a really nice person.

My original distaste for the work may have derived from my thwarted expectation. Now I am glad to own it. Many visitors consider the Driscoll sculpture outstanding. Some mistakenly attribute it to the more famous artist Tony Cragg.

Carol Hepper

My first exposure to Carol Hepper's work was her show at the Cincinnati Contemporary Art Center. At the time, she used stretched animal hides and osier branches to produce quite original results. It echoed her origins, as she was raised on a Western ranch.

I met her for the first time in 1993 when she had another exhibit at the Soma Gallery in downtown San Diego. By then she had changed her style radically and was using flexible copper tubing, anchored by black plumber's elbows, to make swirling, airy shapes that were enormously attractive.

At her opening, I broached Carol about a possible commission, so she came to the house and selected a site, diagonally across and up the path a bit from Ellen Driscoll's cornucopia, waxing very enthusiastic about our project. We spent most of a day together and rapidly found ourselves in synch. She is a most intelligent, agreeable and sympathetic person, whom I would like having as a friend.

Upon her return to New York, she made a sketch of the proposed piece and, after my approbation, started to work expeditiously. A couple of months later I saw the completed sculpture in her studio and was delighted. Then, upon its arrival in La Jolla, she flew to California to supervise the installation—a rather simple matter. In twenty-four hours the ground had been prepared and the cement base poured; after placement of the piece, a gardener replanted a small area and the job was done.

I feel a sense of embarrassment at reporting such a mundane outcome involving a wonderful work of art.

From start to finish, I had unalloyed pleasure in dealing with Carol Hepper. If there had been snags or frustrations I'd have a longer tale to recount about my copper swirls.

Ilan Averbuch

Several years ago on a visit to New York, my wife and I, together with friends Ching Ming and David Grogan, spent a leisurely day in Long Island City—a spot known to too few New Yorkers. It has great Greek restaurants and specialty shops to browse; there are many giant movie sound studios and an outstanding cinema museum. Not far from that is the Isamu Noguchi Museum, overcrowded with examples of his multifaceted career.

Quite nearby is the enormous studio of Mark Di Suvero, combined with the impressive gallery of his longtime dealer, Richard Bellamy, where the public is hospitably received. Adjacent is a large field containing recently completed or partially finished monumental Di Suvero sculptures. Next to *that* is Socrates Park, a public venue for the display of work by young, emerging artists; the city rotates these temporary exhibits perhaps twice a year.

258

A lot of overlooked ability can be seen at Socrates Park for the first time! The four of us were impressed in particular by the power of one series of giant stone arches, created by Ilan Averbuch, which we discussed endlessly on the ride back to Manhattan.

Six months later, I stopped by to greet Sique Spence, director of the Nancy Hoffman Gallery on West Broadway, and was surprised to find a show featuring the work of Averbuch. Discerningly, they too had admired his ability; the public had responded gratifyingly to his first exhibit and newspaper critics gave positive reviews.

A day later, Sique unnecessarily gave me the red carpet treatment by hiring a limousine to drive us to Brooklyn for a studio visit. As she predicted, I found Ilan to be a real charmer, whom I liked immediately. He is a tall, handsome fellow, with a warm, engaging personality. Born in Israel, he had served in the military as a youth and later emigrated to New York, although always maintaining close ties with his native land.

Most of Averbuch's sculptures are massive in size and their scale would be totally unsuitable for an intimate garden, so while he had great work in progress, I found nothing suitable for my purposes. Yet I seemed to pique

259

his interest when he learned which sculptors I had already commissioned, and he consented to pay me a visit in California.

Soon afterward he came to La Jolla and chose a location near the gate of the lower garden. After providing me with sketches of his proposal, he proceeded to construct the piece in his New York studio and returned to supervise installation. Perhaps insultingly, I refer to it as another bird bath (besides the Poiriers'), since it contains water for the neighborhood birds.

The sculpture, titled *Three Wishes*, consists of three identical elements nestling against each other in a zig-zag pattern. Each vertical section is formed of six-inch laminated redwood, six by three feet. The top has been rounded off to make an arc and within each structure are carved three petal shapes, resembling fat fleurs-de-lis. Halfway up each section are four horizontal granite troughs, roughly in the shape of a four-leaf clover, sealed and interconnected, so that they are watertight. With great ingenuity, the heavy stones are supported by metal brackets that lie concealed underneath. All twelve carved granite pieces abut each other, creating the illusion that they might be a single carved slab. The total effect is quite startling and Ilan did a heroic job in working on a modest scale to which he was unaccustomed.

We have since become personal friends and he comes occasionally to visit, or we see each other in New York. Lately I purchased an important LARGE work, which I am donating to the Tel Aviv Museum, since Ilan very much wanted to have an important piece placed in Israel.

David Nash

Around the corner from our Greene Street loft, a new building constructed specifically for art galleries came into being after a few years' delay. One day in early May I entered 130 Prince Street, wandering from floor to floor.

What electrified me was a show of sculptor David Nash at the Louver Gallery (a branch of L.A. Louver in Venice). I had never heard of the man, but here was truly great talent and I could visualize immediately a superb garden piece. As I recall, everything was made of wood, derived from parts of trees, and on top of that were a series of enchanting oil pastel drawings! A brief bio revealed that Nash lived in Wales and had shown extensively with reputable dealers in Europe.

I introduced myself to an employee at the front desk and inquired as to how I might contact the artist. With exemplary caution, she refused to give me the information, but took down my name and address, saying I would hear from their Los Angeles headquarters. Within a few weeks I did receive a call from L.A. about my interest in David Nash. He would be on the West Coast in October for a show and might have a free moment to pay me a call.

In the months that followed, I was in continuous contact with L.A. as his schedule kept changing, but I adjusted myself to suit the artist's convenience. I had the unpleasant feeling that I would be entertaining British "royalty" and not be up to the task. Yet finally D-day arrived and the gallery director, Kimberly Davis, informed me they would be at my house at one o'clock.

I admit to being compulsively punctual and mistakenly hold high expectations for others to behave likewise. To me, tardiness is the ultimate egotistical sin. When two o'clock came without a sign of my visitors, I was steaming. By three o'clock, I was furious and at four o'clock I left for my beloved Thursday afternoon bridge game, which I had previously renounced in the name of ART.

No sooner had I sat down to cool off by playing a rubber than a phone call announced that I had guests awaiting me at home. Tarrying a bit, although the bridge game broke up almost immediately, I returned to the house in a foul mood, determined *not* to receive the wayward travelers.

I have been told that I can look quite forbidding when sufficiently riled, so Kimberly and David divined astutely that I was less than pleased at their presence. Subtly I suggested that since dusk would soon come and they intended to return to L.A. that day, perhaps it would be better if they come back another year. Kimberly muttered a weak apology and David asked what might be amiss. Obviously he was unaware of their schedule.

David asked if he might spend the night and inspect the premises in leisurely fashion the next day, after which he would take the train back to L.A. When I agreed, somewhat begrudgingly, he curtly dismissed crestfallen Kimberly.* When left alone with me, he ex-

---

*With admirable courage, Kimberly Davis paid me a visit some time after our first unfortunate encounter. I found her intelligent and delightful, indeed quite easy to forgive. As a result, I purchased a major painting of the estimable artist John Walker from L.A. Louver, destined for the opening of the La Jolla Museum's new downtown space.

plained that the day's schedule had been unknown to him. At noon they had had lunch and tarried with collector Matt Strauss who had previously purchased one of David's works. When he learned of our one o'clock appointment, he blushed with embarrassment and stuttered an apology. (David has a slight stammer, particularly when upset.) Then he assured me that if we agreed upon a commissioned work, L.A. Louver would be out of the loop and he would deal directly with me at all times. That assurance mollified me greatly, because usually a gallery is an unnecessary interference between the artist and client involved in a specific project.

With the air cleared, we got acquainted during a relaxed dinner and late night chat. My family found him totally engaging, and I liked the twinkle in his eye as well as his sly, low-keyed sense of humor. He confessed that his wife and he were totally committed to a Waldorf School in their poor, slate mining village, so we found in common our admiration for Rudolf Steiner. The community had adopted his educational theories (a competitor to Montessori) and had a large organic garden, with companion planting, mulching, etc., according to his detailed instructions. David and his wife,

Claire, gave much of their spare time to expanding the physical layout of the Snowdonia Steiner School and, in addition, taught there and gave whatever expendable income they could afford in further support. Their dedication seemed refreshing in contrast to the mercenary art scene that exists in America!

Indeed our final arrangement called for me to pay David's direct expenses and his usual fee would be waived. Instead I would contribute an equivalent sum to the Rudolf Steiner Foundation in behalf of the Snowdonia School. So he made no money whatsoever.

In the morning David tramped about the property, photographing potential spots for a sculpture. He then sketched a few preliminary ideas on a scratch pad, saying that he would provide more specific drawings upon his return home. I was startled to find that the final selection of a sculpture depended entirely on what type and shape of tree I found for him to carve, so I became an integral player in the process, which held a certain allure.

From that moment on, I found David Nash to be the most precise, meticulous person I had ever met. Shortly after his return home, I received a loose-leaf book containing photos of potential sites, linked to suggested sculptures for each one. Some called for a hunk of red-wood, others demanded a gum tree, such as eucalyptus. In each case, the exact dimensions of the required wood were given. One strict caveat was that the tree had to be dead or dying; David refused to desecrate anything living. Pages of oil pastel drawings explicated the various shapes available for me to choose. (Each one could be framed as a stunning work of art.) Finally, there was a long memorandum of understanding, outlining exactly our roles, the timing, and the precise costs. It struck a favorable chord with someone trained as a businessman!

The family mulled over our many seductive options, with daughter Nicole leaning toward a sinuous, undulating, six-foot "canoe." But we finally chose a tall "ladder" to be constructed from an entire eucalyptus tree, which would be placed appropriately between two live ones of the same species on a small slope in the lower garden. David approved of our selection enthusiastically and told me to fax him a photograph of a suitable candidate when we found one.

It was then late October 1990, and the artist would return in late April to accomplish the job. The task didn't sound too difficult: I had to find a tree with a clear trunk rising eight feet from the ground, at which point twin sets of branches each would form a "V" of two branches, which in turn grew into a further set of "Vs." In the months that followed, I became the greatest authority alive on the configuration of eucalyptus trees in San Diego County. There was no shortage, live or dead, but nothing came close to what David needed.

I would drive about aimlessly for hours on end, hoping to spot the right specimen. Then, ever resourceful, I enlisted the help of a friend who served on the Park Board, as well as the groundskeeper of UCSD, where the trees grow like weeds. Ironically, after a thundershower, one evening I passed by the La Jolla post office, where lightning had struck two giants. The limbs blocked the street and sanitation crews were preparing to cut down the beauties and clean up the mess. To my astonishment, one of them perfectly fit the description of what I had so long sought. In fact, God had even helped by stripping away much of the foliage. I approached the foreman of the crew and explained that I would pay handsomely for it if he left the trunk and certain branches intact. Either he could deliver the tree to my home nearby, or early the next day I would hire someone to haul it away. Savagely, he spurned my entreaty and rather succinctly told me to bugger off, as he had work to do and had to meet his boss's deadline. He thought I was another local weirdo, and ignored my fervent plea.

Time marched on inexorably toward the fateful date of David's arrival and I was getting quite desperate by late February. In the meantime, I had engaged the services of Matthieu Gregoire, assistant to Mary Beebe at the UCSD sculpture garden, who would act as coordinator in behalf of David Nash. Matthieu had many resources at his command, since he had overseen installation of complex, monumental sculptures on numerous occasions. Besides, he was a fine sculptor himself, who understood an artist's mentality.

One bright day in March, Matthieu telephoned to report that he had found the perfect tree on campus. It had died under siege by some ravaging insect and was slated for the axe. He had prevailed upon the proper authorities to delay its execution a month, until David Nash could supervise the removal. Immediately, I took a Polaroid shot of the tree and faxed it to Wales for approval. With a sigh of relief, I got back posthaste the proper endorsement for our choice.

David sent Matthieu a detailed list of what he would require in the way of equipment and supplies, as well as a precise time line for completion of the sculpture: i.e., dismemberment would commence at 7:00 A.M., April 18; on-site creation of the piece thereafter until noon on the 19th, when he had to leave for Los Angeles. Installation would occur upon his return on the 20th, with an extra day's leeway, if necessary. I stood in awe of such precision planning—even Matthieu seemed a bit skeptical that the project would be created so expeditiously.

Nash arrived the evening of the 17th with his experienced assistant, Charles Lindner (also a sculptor), and his young friend. They checked out Matthieu and found everything ready and to their satisfaction.

Early the next morning, a crane and flatbed truck arrived at UCSD for the operation, as I gazed in wonderment at the flawless execution of the plan. After trimming the tree at the university, they brought the trunk and remaining limbs on the flatbed to my garden gate. Inside, on a flat area, the sculpting began immediately. David's principal tool is a chainsaw that has as many blades as a golf bag has clubs. He has a wizard's grasp of what the saw can do; the team of three worked nonstop until the following noon, bringing the "ladder" to realization.

In the interim, I could make no sense out of the components that came into being until I saw the completed sculpture in place the following day. During construction Matthieu proved invaluable in his unobtrusive way, supplying block and tackle, chains, ropes—whatever might have been overlooked appeared like magic in no time. He became an integral member of a smooth-working team.

The final installation was itself a work of art: Four holes had been dug in the hillside and filled with gravel; each was to accommodate one "leg" of the structure. After the huge, weighty monster had been dragged to the site, the piece was raised by block and tackle (attached to the sturdy limb of an adjacent tree) and, magically, the towering sculpture stood perfectly erect in the proper spot. What masterful engineering!

David's "ladder" stands some twenty feet high. The core of the tree was removed at the outset. (This created a separate, graceful, free-standing sculpture that stands in the corner of my living room.) The remains of the tree were upended so that the four branches became the "legs" of the piece, each irregular in length, to accommodate the slope, and extending about ten feet off the ground. Above are four evenly spaced rungs that hold the two separate sections of the main trunk firmly together.

It is a spectacular piece and, interestingly enough, it is enhanced by the work of the insects that had destroyed the eucalyptus. They had bored under the bark, creating fascinating paths along the surface that became exposed when the cortex was removed. David created a masterpiece in a time span that I would have considered impossible, had I not witnessed it personally.

In early June 1992, I paid David and Claire a call. I felt it important to visit someone with the following address:

Capel Rhiw, Blaenau Ffestiniog,
Gwynedd, North Wales, LL41 3NT

I found the Nashes living in a drab, former slate mining town, a veritable desert in the picturesque oasis that comprises northern and central Wales. They reside in a deconsecrated church, which serves as a splendid studio and home. David needs a lot of room for his work, so he found the perfect location. The place is crammed with completed sculptures, as well as works in process. To the rear is a spacious garden, where he can sculpt part of the year, and there is a large supply of special wood that he has scrounged over the years for future use. Behind that is an enormous mountain of discarded slate shards that must have built up over *centuries*. The depressing pile must reach several hundred feet in height; seemingly over time the Nashes have become impervious to the view, since it didn't elicit a single comment. In sharp contrast, across the street from the "church," David has built a new drawing studio that is modern and impeccably designed—singularly out of place in those environs.

A writer for *Contemporanea* magazine once quoted David as saying: "As a student I realized that the aesthetic I had was very small, and the aesthetic in nature was enormous." When he drove us into the countryside to show his proudest achievements, I better understood what he meant. We went down a lane, off the highway, to a bridge centuries old. A short distance upstream he showed us what appeared to be a granite boulder, nestled among others. Yet a close inspection revealed it to

272

be made of oak. In 1978, David had chopped a segment from the trunk of a fallen oak tree and placed it quite a distance upstream. Over the years it had slowly drifted downward, buffeted by rock and water, until it had become almost perfectly spherical with time. Possibly it had reached its final destination, or maybe it would tumble further along. During all this time, David has regularly documented the evolution of his *Wooden Boulder*.

Afterwards we drove miles further into the country and finally stopped in the middle of nowhere. David explained that he had bought property at this spot years before and we would be viewing his favorite project. So we traipsed through overgrown fields, fighting our way through bramble thickets to arrive at a clearing, where we found twenty-two ash trees—that had been planted in 1977—in a wide circle. Apologetically, he explained that this was a thirty-year project and only half the time had elapsed. He had been carefully pruning, notching and bending the saplings so they would eventually co-join in what he called his *Ash Dome*. The effect was startling as the trees seemed to bow toward each other; evidently he was well on his way to realizing a dream of combining his talent with the growth of natural forces.

273

I saw clearly a compulsive/obsessive personality, engulfed in an ongoing struggle to achieve a strange ambition. His commitment demanded constant supervision and cultivation to bend the will of nature to his ends.

The Debacles

Although I found myself somewhat debilitated by the contretemps with Michael Singer, the constant gastroenterological problems of Ann Preston's "Peepee," and the medical bills from the Pond Doctor for keeping Alice Aycock's "Moorish Fantasy" on life support, I now realize that such disappointments were trivial compared to what followed. It was the later debacles that led me to renounce forever the commissioning of garden sculpture.

Mary Miss

Mary Miss has been well recognized as a prominent artist for more than twenty-five years. In the early 1980s her dealer, Max Protetch, showed me a slide carousel of her work from the '60s, and one was more spectacular than the others, so I ended up buying an impressive sculpture that I was happy to own. For some unaccountable reason her discrete works didn't sell well, but she was reputed to make a good living by teaching and realizing many commissions for public institutions. I recall seeing her exciting show at the Whitechapel in London that justifiably received rave review in the local press.

I felt it would be fabulous to have a project with Mary Miss, so I was delighted when she agreed to pay a visit in the late spring of 1991. She proved to be an exceptional person: With erect posture and perfectly chiseled features, she has the bearing of a princess. Poised and low-keyed, she engenders immediate respect, and one has the impression that her waters run deep. I felt awe in her presence. After her visit, she wrote of her pleasure contemplating our collaboration and I was all puffed up at her remarks: "Your place is quite remarkable between its physical location and the artworks."

As I peruse our correspondence and think back on our infrequent telephone conversations, I feel a sinking depression. They record an artist and a client, living in totally different worlds, failing to communicate—a situation that can only lead to disaster. To me words have precise meaning; presumably, to certain artists, they have an elasticity. It demands a lot of patron flexibility.

Mary returned to La Jolla in November that year and chose a specific site, up the hill above *The Islands of the Moons and Suns* in a wooded area, where there was a fine view of the ocean. She and I envisioned a "meditation" spot where a simple structure would be appropriate. Since there was no easy access, we considered a zigzag path, possibly constructed of railroad ties, with a rope handrail.

At that time we discussed a budget that would leave me with peace of mind. Mary mentioned a total cost of $15,000–20,000, plus her fee adding considerably more, to which I assented. On the side of caution I confirmed the lower figure, but in reply she stated that she would be much more comfortable with an additional sum: "It seems that $25,000 is a more realistic figure. I am basing this response on intuition rather than facts, but I would be more comfortable estimating high rather than surprising you later." The numbers escalated early on.

We further agreed that the project would be completed within one year and, if for any reason we didn't go through with the plan, she would still receive a fee of $5,000. In return for that amount, she proffered a drawing or another work pertaining to the project. As I look back, I can't think of how our understanding was flawed; it seemed to encompass the major points quite specifically.

One thing arose immediately: Mary would need a land survey prior to drawing her plans. So I hired David Singer, a top architect, and a surveyor. Although an unexpected expense, it didn't seem material. At the end of 1991, all was ready to go and I awaited word from the artist.

Mary Miss is another sculptor much in demand with constituencies to whom she is answerable. Time passed and I'd receive an odd postcard apologizing for the delays. Finally, in March 1993, I got photographs of a maquette and architectural drawings from her (which I read with difficulty). The proposal seemed rather more elaborate than I would have expected, but if she could realize it within our budget, I would be more than gratified. I confirmed my pleasure at the design in a telephone call to her and she said that the final budget would be forthcoming.

Two months later the budget arrived in the mail. The

277

direct construction cost came to just shy of *double* the original maximum of $25,000! This failed to take into account other expenses, such as demolition of solar panels on the site, construction of the path and extensive landscaping, which I estimated could run an additional $10,000–15,000. No contingency reserve had been calculated and, from experience, I know the slightest snag or miscalculation can be dreadfully expensive. In her cover letter, Mary seemed to indicate that the estimate had been higher but, by cutting various corners, she had reduced it to the final amount. At the end of her missive, she suggested that we have a phone call to discuss the matter.

After mulling over the contents of the budget for a few days, I decided that any conversation would be futile—it only could lead to argument or recrimination—so I spent hours composing a letter, by which I terminated any further development of the project. We seemed so far apart that no compromise would be feasible, particularly since the sum had been REDUCED already. I believe I couched my sentiments in the polite, respectful terms due to such a fine artist.

The telephonic response I got to my letter had my ears ringing for days; I had provoked a torrent of vituperation, which I accepted mutely. Shortly afterwards, I received a calm note from her that delineated quite accurately how we two lived in worlds apart. She had felt the "final budget" was a starting point and between the two of us we would have found a point of accommodation and compromise. Graciously she added: "You have been patient in waiting for my proposal, and I cannot fault you for misunderstanding the budget." She ended up by recommending that I should better understand an artist's mentality in the future.

Always having the last word, I wrote Mary Miss a final letter which I ended by saying:

"While this is the first time I have had such a negative time with an artist, I want you to know that it sufficiently depressed me that I am swearing off any future collaboration. When it is no longer pleasant, I quit.

"This does not in any way mean that I blame you; it is just that at my age I don't need negative experiences and I don't want to be responsible for inadvertently causing hurt to good people."

Maria Nordman

What transpired with Mary Miss was a lighthearted romp compared to my involvement with Maria Nordman. Just the thought of what happened leaves me quivering with anger and frustration. She caused me to finally realize that I am just a client of artists, one who dishes out the coin of the realm for what they produce. I am unlike museum curators and dealers, who are paid to pamper and cater to artistic temperaments. On occasion a museum director will cavil to an arrogant painter or sculptor when *murder* would have been the more appropriate response!

My downfall came through the good offices of my friend Marian Goodman, who had already arranged for sculptures by Giuseppe Penone and Dan Graham to adorn my garden. She explained what I already knew from hearsay that Maria Nordman was highly "important" in today's art panoply and added that she sorely needed money. Apparently Marian wanted to cure Maria's financial malaise at one stroke; the fee would be hefty. My advisor assured me that my act would validate my reputation as a true connoisseur and I'd "never regret the decision." With these famous last words, a deal was struck.

In my profession as a psychologist I have developed a high threshold of tolerance for irrationality in others. My expectations for sane behavior are strictly limited.

In the case of Maria Nordman, I'm ashamed to report that late in the game I totally lost my cool. I admit that my reactions are obviously highly subjective.

Maria, impervious to any negativity she engenders, blithely goes on her way, apparently deluding herself that she will go down in history as one of the greatest artists of our time. Sadly, she must be frustrated that there is little of hers in public venues to go down through the ages. This derives in part from her making temporary installations which are dismantled soon after display. Moreover, she does not kindle a warmth that would lead donors and museums to extend themselves in her behalf; quite contrarily, I've heard her state unalterable terms and conditions that would preclude almost any institution from accepting a gift of her work, much less buy one. As her name arose among my acquaintances in the art world, it became evident that others had had difficult experiences although she had so many loving and loyal friends. She cut a destructive path among the personnel of art galleries and museums. Several people, requesting anonymity, told me that if they ever were called upon to work with her again, they would go on strike or quit before suffering a repeat performance.

All this notwithstanding, Maria has been greatly

sought after for years, and has traveled widely making her installation pieces, doing performances and readings, as well as proselytizing her mesmerized converts. Maria, now a cult figure, has even Marian Goodman under her spell.

When Maria did an installation at the La Jolla Museum of Contemporary Art in February 1985 (*Trabajos En La Ciudad De Ondas*), I found it banal and humorless despite its serious intensity. Still, the erudite and well-respected chief curator, Ron Onorato, wrote a six-page paean of praise in the catalogue as he reviewed her crowning achievements over the previous fifteen years.

Prior to the monograph is a quotation that reminds me of Gertrude Stein in its profundity:

> A work is open.
> A work is open to consideration.
> A work is open to consideration for placement.
> —*Maria Nordman, working notes, 1980*

Onorato describes in detail the composition of "De Ondas" and proceeds to provide vividly the essence of the artist's work. To quote out of context—but, it is hoped, with some accuracy—I offer:

Nordman has, for more than a decade, created open-ended situations where her audience can share various effects of natural light in its dialogue with man-made structures.

De Ondas acts as a conduit for people, light, air and other elements of its environment.

Nordman does not create REPRESENTA-TIONS of things in the outside world but PRE-SENTATIONS of opportunities for us to consider that world through our senses.

. . . Nordman is as involved with other sensate aspects of the environment—not just light, shadow, temperature, color, tactility and scale of spatial comprehension, but the sociological and human presence that inevitably surrounded her art as well.

. . . Nordman proceeds from effect toward cause, from sense to object and, ultimately, from a concept of what is perceivable toward its physical means.

As a visual artist Nordman operates on (and we as members of her audience follow) an empirical method where the thingness of art as commodity is superseded by an investigatory process channeled through our perceptive faculties.

As an art collector, I admit to not making heads or tails of "artspeakdeconstructtexticism" and although I subscribe to four principal art magazines and for years would read the texts with diligent studiousness, I could never really grasp content and gradually limited myself to my two favorite art critics, Anne Rorimer and Robert Hughes.

In the case of Ron Onorato, I wasn't really sure what he was saying, but I got the idea that Maria Nordman wasn't too interested in making works of art per se, but instead wanted to stimulate the senses of the viewer in more esoteric, oblique ways. *De Ondas* was bridge-like, or rather, a well-crafted tunnel that extended from a gallery through a door in the outside wall of the museum. At the exterior were several panels, covered with brightly painted canvas. While others gushed, my private judgment gave the structure "E" for effort.

When Marian Goodman first broached the idea of a commission, my only point of reference was the La Jolla piece that I had seen five years before. I attributed my own lack of enthusiasm to a want of sensibility. When I expressed a gnawing doubt that a Nordman piece would be appropriate for my garden, Marian chided me for my narrow definition of contemporary art and challenged me to widen my horizons. This would be a daring "happening" that would stretch my mind and afford both me and the public great pleasure. So she laid down the irresistible gauntlet.

In hindsight, I recognize that a fair measure of the anger I direct at Maria should be pointed inwardly at myself. I took leave of my aesthetic sensibility by minimizing my lack of interest in *De Ondas* and I took leave of my senses when I permitted any artist to assume full control of what would eventually come into my possession. With docility I accepted a plan which I never fully understood until the time of installation. Certainly Marian Goodman's encouragement contributed to my passivity.

Ms. Nordman paid her first visit to La Jolla in early autumn 1992. Although she is not conventionally attractive, her eyes have a certain sparkle and she is garrulous to a fault. Often, though, she did not make much sense and her voice, perhaps due to throat tension, has a squeaky, abrasive quality that immediately set my nerves on edge.

After perusing the property, Maria settled upon a site at the bottom of the lower garden, where a hideous chain-link fence opened onto the rear lane. She wished to replace it with a more appropriate gate and utilize space directly in front of it for other elements. What she saw was a project with two facets: one situated on my land, the other in a public place; together they would form an important gestalt. She liked the idea of Nicole's school as public place, and possibly the Salk Institute as an alternative option. That day we canvassed the two possibilities and she couldn't decide which she preferred, they were both so suitable (of course, reckoning without our hosts).

Maria took measurements of the area and we discussed a budget of $15,000, which didn't seem out of line. I vaguely grasped at the concept of the two sites being inextricably linked, which left me a bit uncomfortable. I told her I didn't wish to have the responsibility of finding other venues or coordinating efforts between us. Also, I demurred when she requested that I make a pitch to the Bishop's School and Salk Institute, as I felt that she thoroughly understood the project and I didn't. So we agreed that she would make presentations at a future date and I would be excluded from a role in the matter. Big mistake.

We parted ways and I heard little or nothing from Maria until early February, when she requested a remittance be sent to her fabricator, who was ready to start constructing the work. It would be completed by early May, when she would come to supervise installation. At the outset, she had informed me that she worked on only one project at a time, so I was highly elated that for once a "sculpture" would be completed in timely fashion.

Indeed, on the first of May an impressive array of large crates appeared, which I stacked up in the garage, thereby displacing a vehicle. Maria came up with some lame excuse that she would be delayed until June—and later pushed her visit off until July. When she finally appeared it was for a hurried visit of a few hours; she had to be here, she had to be there and it would be impossible to erect the piece until September.

We paid a call upon Hugh Davies and, with curator Kathryn Kanjo present, the two discussed the possibility of showing the new work at the museum. I sat dumbfounded as I listened to a surreal conversation: After Hugh expressed interest in displaying the work from November through year-end, Maria insisted it would only be acceptable to her if the museum produced a catalogue and gave widespread publicity. Hugh patiently explained that her demands could not be met. The galleries would be shutting down for a two-year renovation in December; there was neither staff nor funds available to achieve her wishes.

Maria believes in the power of words—obviously, the *more* the better. To each constraint that Hugh Davies brought up, she had a ready riposte. And she returned again and again. With saintly forbearance, Hugh kept stressing his respect for her sublime art and her as a person, still stoutly standing his ground. They were in a verbal minuet which dragged on for symphonic length with no resolution. Finally Maria flounced out of the room in a huff, with me trailing behind. I was astonished that in the car she appeared highly *gratified* at the meeting, commenting how *well* she and Hugh Davies got along.

Immediately afterwards we visited the Bishop's School, where Maria met with the headmaster, the head of the art department, and other personnel to propose installing Part A of my commissioned work (after the La Jolla Museum shut down—although that seemed a rather optimistic assumption). If they clearly understood what she explained, they were one up on me; her prattling was unintelligible, in my opinion, but they acted quite respectfully, possibly not wanting to offend a parent (me) who contributed tidy sums in addition to the hefty tuition. Everyone agreed to pursue the matter further in the autumn, but nothing concrete ever resulted from the meeting.

Maria then disappeared for three months, surfacing anew on October 17 with the first of a series of lengthy faxes that splattered out of my machine over the next few days. She had suddenly become a whirlwind of activity, having come to an agreement with the La Jolla Museum for the display of Part A during November and December; her non-negotiable demands had melted away, as pragmatically she accepted the terms originally enunciated by Hugh Davies.

At that point she decided that I must sign a contract containing detailed demands about my future performance. With the precision of a finely honed legal mind, paragraphs explicated my future role and responsibilities. Ex post facto, after I had advanced a substantial amount eight months earlier, she now arbitrarily came up with eerie stipulations:

The agreement would be binding on any future owner of the work. Two locations could be chosen only "with the cooperation of choice of location with Maria Nordman."

The precise location of this work is chosen with Maria Nordman.

The inset parts of the structure are taken out in the same time in one place with the other . . .

The elements inset into the wall of this work are taken out in harmony of time with the elements situated in the public building.

The contract then went on in great detail, stipulating that during her absence, if a new site were selected:

A Polaroid of the work is sent to her before showing. All sites are photographed with the specifications of Maria Nordman, with the film and all prints belonging to her . . .

The exterior work is oiled once a year with a natural oil.

The paint, should it be damaged, will be painted with the same color acrylic as the first painting, and be documented by a curator of painting from the museum. (A similar clause pertained to replacement of the Oregon cedar.)

Clearly, I would be unable to display my Part B unless Part A was shown *simultaneously*—and there was no sign of a permanent home for it. Also, I'd be responsible for the maintenance of both in perpetuity, although one was out of my control. To live up to the terms, I would require a full-time curator. Summarily I refused to sign and Maria refused to come to La Jolla.

We both stuck fast, until Marian Goodman interceded (as she did frequently in the days that followed) and suggested "a best efforts" clause, which resolved the problem; however, Maria had me add: "Further, I shall instruct my executor [son Eddie] to take on the same task, or any future owner or museum." Maria had in mind that the cedar could last an easy five hundred years and was hereby ensuring that her work would endure in posterity.

In the reams of paper received that week, I got an inkling of what the piece was about: "With six insets, when folded out, having various states, one state is potentially in reference to a house—a table, four chairs and a bed. The meaning of the work is not predetermined, and is to stay open, not for a particular repetitive use." A few days later, when the crates were finally opened, lo and behold, the elements strongly resembled a bridge table, four square stools and a low-slung, simple coffee table rather than a bed.

291

My Part B had six items with plywood surfaces, which, when the legs were folded, nestled cunningly into the $12' \times 6'$ wooden slatted gate. The six identical components of Part A had canvas tops painted in acrylic primary colors. These fit into another $12' \times 6'$ frame, which had white painted canvas on one side. In the museum installation, the large white expanse contrasted well against the bright colors of the six brightly hued elements, although personally I found the work uninspiring and banal.

Nordman's Installation

By coincidence, Maria Nordman had an opening at the Margo Leavin Gallery on Saturday, October 23. Responding to Margo's gracious invitation to a dinner party afterwards at her home, I planned a trip to Los Angeles. My friend Erika Hartman, owner of an excellent La Jolla art gallery, accompanied me and we had a pleasant and successful day.

We arrived at the Margo Leavin Gallery just as Maria was finishing a performance. I still have written excerpts of that unintelligible gibberish.

Daylight was fading fast (Maria insists on only natural light), but we distinguished many elements strewn about the gallery, some of which strongly resembled those that I would view at my house a couple of days later. The installation made absolutely no sense to me, but I knew I should be admiring it.

The dinner at Margo's was the epitome of what I imagine a Beverly Hills party should be. Her immaculate, spacious home is a perfect showcase for art and has a spectacular view of the valley below. Margo had thoughtfully seated me beside Maria, one of two guests of honor (the other was Joseph Kosuth, who had a concurrent opening in Margo Leavin's second gallery building).

Understandably, Maria was quite high after her success, but later her energy flagged and she decided not to return to La Jolla with us, as originally planned. Instead she would fly down the following evening and be ready for work early Monday morning. In a few days she was due in Germany for a teaching commitment; before that she had the L.A. opening AND had to prepare Part A for the La Jolla Museum (and, hopefully, my Part B as well). She loaded up my car with cans of paint and various tools at Margo's, and twenty-four hours later I met her at the San Diego airport.

Originally it had been contemplated that Maria

would supply her own experienced workmen to assemble the items in my garage but, as the time grew near, for some unaccountable reason she had no one available. Her ready solution was that *I* should find someone—who had to be a master carpenter, due the fragility of the elements. The only problem was that I didn't know one, and I didn't want the responsibility for hiring a person who might make a hash of the job. I did know a home repair contractor whose carpenter had done odd jobs around the house quite competently, but I could scarcely vouch for the degree of skill this assignment seemed to entail. (Maria's reply: "Bob, you're always so negative.")

There appeared to be no other viable option, so I put Maria in touch with the contractor, with whom she arranged to have two people available early Monday morning. Presumably she was satisfied with their qualifications.

Bright and early, Mike and his assistant, Wayne, appeared. By a miracle, they both proved to be experienced and masterful in their abilities. In fact, later Maria pronounced them both the most accomplished men with whom she had ever worked (a thought not reciprocated by them).

As the men started opening the many crates, our nightmare began. Before they had finished unwrapping the elements, Maria announced that they had better speed up the pace, since she intended to depart late that afternoon; at that Mike said they would quit immediately, since they knew too little to proceed without her. In consternation, I headed for the telephone to call Marian Goodman, who interceded and forcefully told the artist that she was to remain until the piece was installed. Evidently Marian is the only one to whom she will listen. I eavesdropped, hearing: "Yes, Marian, O.K. Marian. Yes, I promise." All in an unusually docile tone of voice.

She remained until Wednesday noon, creating constant havoc as she gave incessant instructions and then countermanded them. Those hours remain indelible in my mind, but in addition I kept a diary by means of which I hoped to dissipate my mounting ire. My time was mostly spent mollifying the workmen to keep them on the job (at $70 per hour).

Maria decided she wanted to have a lengthy description of the piece burnt into each of the two parts by laser etcher, so she took off with Mike to a distant suburb with a component strip of wood which proved to be too narrow. They took a wider strip on a second trip, thereby wasting most of the morning. By dusk Mike had had it and refused to return the next day, so Wayne, with a higher tolerance for erratic behavior, stayed on doggedly throughout. When Maria left at noon Wednesday, Wayne understood what was needed to complete the job and Mike immediately reappeared. With a sense of relief, they labored efficiently together for a couple of days, undoing her faulty suggestions and redoing until the gate was installed and the museum's Part A was ready to be picked up. Maria haunted us even in her absence, bombarding us with faxes in the following days and calling Wayne incessantly at home, giving conflicting orders. At 10:30 P.M. Thursday he disconnected his telephone.

When I first gazed at the elements lying on the garage floor, I saw the most outstanding craftsmanship I could ever imagine. While I found Maria's creation uninteresting, the woodworker, Makoto Imai, is an artist and craftsman of premier rank. The white cedar glistened with a superb patina and there wasn't a nail or screw anywhere. Everything had perfect pegs in a tongue and groove construction. The latticed gate looked wonderful, resting on the brown composite stone. This temporarily softened my feeling toward Maria, as I anticipated a happy conclusion that would make all the previous aggravation worthwhile.

Unfortunately this early assessment proved premature, because, upon final installation, I saw it all quite differently. When erected, the gate appeared rather ordinary, as the undistinguished background of the adjacent lane appeared. (A two-edged sword: The neighbors could peer inside my garden.) The plain plywood stools, table and "bed" placed randomly on the gravel in front of the gate—per the artist's instructions—offered no visual gratification whatsoever. In fact, they *detracted* from what I had tried so hard to achieve over the years.

Meanwhile, the La Jolla Museum installed Part A and it looked quite a bit better. The strong primary colors on the surfaces of that furniture added a lot, particularly when juxtaposed to a 12′ × 6′ white expanse. It was not a crowd-stopper, but Hugh Davies and his curatorial staff seemed delighted.

Determined that Part B would not remain Chez Orton—since I wanted to be rid of it and anything to remind me of the name Maria Nordman—I suggested to Davies that it would be *most appropriate* if the museum owned *both* Parts A and B. Floored by my generosity, he accepted with alacrity, and I wiped my brow with a sigh of relief. So, just after the new year, Part B left my yard forever and I had a nondescript but adequate cedar gate built to replace Maria's. It was not the first time I had made a hideous mistake, but I rejoiced in extricating myself so expeditiously.

One time Maria wrote me that she found "humor in the wood" and, on several occasions, she emphasized that we would have a joyous collaboration. What transpired, however, was definitely *not* joyous. As my wrath mounted at her arrogant intransigence, on Monday afternoon I told her off in no uncertain terms. Uncharacteristically judgmental, I told Maria she was the most *unlovable* person I had ever met, although I still respected her as an artist (flagrant hypocrisy). I added that my ego was fully as strong as hers and warned her not to push me too far. She might keep in mind that I was not a doormat like the dealers and curators, since I, as a private citizen, had employed her and paid the bills. In addition, I expected a moratorium on ultimatums, a cessation of "disinformation," and she might commence performing according to MY expectations.

My unexpected outburst quieted Maria a bit, but not for long.

I skip over the working hours, when Wayne and Mike labored valiantly to paint, stretch canvas and assemble the elements, but Monday evening's events complete the story. Late that afternoon, in one of my many telephonic pleas to Marian Goodman, Marian warned me that I might find Maria Niobe-like, a "weeper" under stress. I expressed my doubts about that, but assured her that, as a therapist, I was accustomed to similar behavior and would keep a Kleenex box handy.

I rued the fact that Maria would join my family and me at an Italian restaurant for supper, but I had also invited Kathryn Kanjo, senior curator of the La Jolla Museum, to join us, since it would be her only opportunity to discuss the logistics of installation of Part A. Until then she had little or no idea of the piece or what might be entailed.

After an enervating day, at 6:00 P.M. I drank a gin and soda to calm my frayed nerves and wrote a few lines in my diary. A half hour later I called Maria to leave, as we were to meet the other three who would arrive separately. She replied that she didn't drive with drinkers and would call a taxi. I remonstrated that the place was but three minutes distant, but she was adamant.

At dinner Maria conducted a monologue directed at the others, reciting her many grievances over the lack of cooperation and ill treatment she had received. I surmised that she was trying to provoke me into a response, but I sat quiet and miserable. Well-trained Kathryn tried to appease her.

Toward the end of the meal, Maria finally addressed me directly:

"Bob, we were supposed to have a joyous experience and it isn't working out that way. I think we should call it quits right now and, to recompense you for the money already spent, I'll give you a couple of valuable drawings."

At that moment, my heart sang with joy and I replied:

"Maria, you have made a splendid suggestion; however, I don't want your drawings under any circumstances, or have anything further to do with you! Certainly it is not my first loss—nor will it be my last."

I could see I had finally gotten to Maria, as her face

dropped and she fled from the table. Those two cowards, my wife and daughter, headed quickly for the door, leaving Kathryn and me alone. Poor Kathryn, totally unaccustomed to direct confrontation, was in a state of shock:

"Bob, how could you? With artists you must . . ."

"Kathryn, never fear. She has the hide of a rhinoceros and I predict she'll soon be back, undaunted and unscathed."

Before long, Maria reappeared (perhaps after a good cry), cheerful and full of smiles:

"Bob, we shouldn't be quarreling like this. We can certainly do better."

"Maria, THAT is entirely up to you!" So we buried the hatchet temporarily.

Kathryn drove Maria back to our house and they had a technical discussion about the "sculpture." Eventually the kindly curator left and Maria asked me to escort her to the second-floor guest quarters, since she was afraid (of what?). Immediately she complained that the horizontally sliding windows lacked a "safety bar," which she always found at the house of her friend Sally Yard. Since evidently Maria was deathly afraid of burglars, I reassured her by pointing out that there was a sheer thirty-foot drop to the ravine below and the most agile cat burglar in the world couldn't scale that wall. Gritting my teeth, I bade Maria good night.

Ten minutes later, I got a signal from Maria on auto-call, which woke everyone in the house. When I rang her station, she whispered that there was a prowler directly outside her bedroom. "Come! Help!" Fearlessly I returned to the carriage house and, upon entering the bedroom, indeed I heard an eerie sound: "Swish, Swish, Swish." Steeling myself courageously, I went outside to investigate. The series of swishes were caused by a sprinkler-head spraying the adjacent area for a fifteen-minute dowsing. My triumphant discovery didn't mollify Maria, so I offered her two options: She could wait five more minutes, until it stopped, or she could move to our second guest house by the tennis court, which had two vacant bedrooms. She grumbled that she'd suffer where she was, but sleep would be out of the question after her shattering experience.

Now that sufficient time has passed, and I am no longer too miffed, I see the "Maria Nordman" episode for what it was: "Opera Buffa" on a grand scale. Since then, I've teased the good-natured Kathryn about her hopeless task of trying to spread sweetness and light between two adversaries locked in mortal combat.

After Maria's departure and the last flurry of faxes, I have never heard again from her and, hopefully, she is out of my life forever.

Regrouping: A Fresh Start

Licking my wounds after recent negative encounters, I've veered in a new direction, developing the ample garden space still available. No more commissions; I purchase sculpture already fabricated—preferably by someone deceased, though that is a bit difficult in the field of contemporary art.

Howard Ben Tre

In September 1993, I flew east to Providence, Rhode Island, to visit Howard Ben Tre, who had an exhibit at the List Gallery of Brown University. Howard is a preeminent sculptor in glass, using a proprietary technique he has developed over the years. His individual work—as well as public commissions—keeps him

303

hopping, leaving him impervious to the notable down-draft in art sales in recent times.

Long ago I met Howard and we stayed in close contact through correspondence; he always had a cogent reason why he could not supply me with a work, but finally my persistence bore fruit. In June 1993 he paid me a visit and after he chose a location for a sculpture, we spent an amicable several days together. Three months later I was proud to own the pick of the litter: *Wrapped Form 4*, 1993. Standing four feet high, it graces the covered terrace facing the swimming pool, since it would be inadvisable to expose it to the weather. I'm grateful for such a painless experience in acquiring beauty.

Jann Haworth

Not many weeks after my trip to Providence, I found myself in London with daughter Robin on a fortnight's jaunt for father and daughter to refresh each other's company. We did a bit of gallery hopping and stopped by Gimpel Fils, a noted spot owned by a dynasty of antiquarians that has been prominent for more than a century. Directly facing the entrance was a single sculpture that compelled our attention (*Lady T*). Eleven feet high, it consisted of thick steel rods that had been twisted into an abstracted human form. The rest of the gallery displayed paintings, all containing explicit references to barbed wire, twisted into ingenious shapes. Obviously the three-dimensional figure played on that motif.

We met the polite, agreeable gallery director, Simon Lee, and learned that the artist had been born and bred in Beverly Hills. Jann Haworth had an early success, showing with the prestigious Sidney Janis Gallery in New York, before she became an expatriate in England. For the past twenty years, Haworth had devoted her life to educating youngsters and developing their artistic abilities. Living in rural obscurity for a generation, she had just recently emerged from her cocoon to produce work for her re-debut.

To encourage sales, Gimpel had set prices more than reasonable by American standards. In fact, the price of the sculpture was so low it must have netted little after deducting the cost of fabrication. I bought it immediately, which seemed to gratify everyone at the gallery, and a couple of months later *Lady T* arrived at my doorstep via ocean shipment.

It was a simple matter to level a small plot of ground which accommodated the steel base-plate of the structure, so the sculpture stands tall and proud in the rose garden that faces my snug office. During recent months I've established a close rapport with gracious *Lady T.*

Andrew Spence and Seth Kaufman

As I come to the denouement of my garden caper, I tend to dwell on the positive aspects of collecting and developing a sculpture garden. Certainly the friendships formed and the people of probity and character I met far outweigh the niggling pettiness that at times wrecked my pleasure. I wrote early on that I always tried to be a positive force in the world of art, so I think back with a smile how, from time to time, I could be very supportive of fledgling artists with little seed money. Thus, on two occasions, I inadvertently became a *vehicular* benefactor.

I met Andy Spence and his wife, Sique, in 1979. Andy was having a hard time making ends meet and often had odd jobs around Soho, such as at Paula Cooper Gallery and Artist's Space—but whenever feasible, he devoted himself to painting. He worked diligently and painstakingly, often reworking a canvas countless times in order to achieve the precise result he wished.

From the outset, I admired Andy's persistence, but

306

more than that he is a wonderful artist. Before he had a regular gallery (he now shows with Max Protetch), I bought a number of his works, several of which I'm proud to have in my home. He paints in a minimalist, geometrical style, with an individual stamp that one can recognize at a glance—also true of our mutual hero, John McLaughlin.

One day I visited his studio and found a freshly completed red painting, totally divergent from his usual format. I made a comment to that effect, saying: "It reminds me of a VW roof." At that Andy burst out laughing and complimented me on my perspicacity. He had been dreaming of a third-hand car he had spotted, but couldn't afford. It would be impractical to own in New York City but still would be great for weekend forays into the countryside. At that, I asked the price of the car, which turned out to be modest indeed, and wrote out a cheque on the spot, adding enough to cover license fees and insurance—and walked away with the "VW" painting.

My second "automotive" experience happened just a few months ago and involved an incredibly talented young fellow—Seth Kaufman, a true Renaissance

307

man: He is a dancer, composer and musician, a most sensitive and articulate writer and, on top of that, a fine sculptor. I met him in Los Angeles—where he has resided for some years—the same day I went to Maria Nordman's opening at Margo Leavin's. My cousin Nancy took me to see his show at a small gallery and to meet the artist.

Seth lived in an area that was the vortex of the Los Angeles riots, which left a deep impression on him. He salvaged many objects from burned-out buildings and incorporated them into compelling sculptures. In addition, he started making collages from the painted metal carcasses of wrecked autos, which he affixed to backboards with rows of bolts. It produced a startling effect. Even more unusual was a tall vertical piece, made of numerous narrow, colored strips from automotive sheaths that he twisted around a central pole. This sculptural element was attached to a fractional motor on the ceiling, which spun it about at a steady, slow speed.

I expressed my fascination with the effect it produced, but I enunciated my quirky aversion to kinetic sculpture (probably derived from recent disasters induced by water and electricity among my garden

308

pieces). Gratuitously I opined that a free-standing sculpture that did *not* rotate might be even more effective. He expressed effusive thanks for the brilliant suggestion of a rich collector and we parted on good terms.

A month later, Seth came to La Jolla to view the garden and pass the time of day. At one point, he muttered that he had a few things in his pickup that he'd like to show me and, upon my request, set them out in our adjacent studio. To my surprise, he had followed my suggestion and I beheld a sculpture about seven feet high that was just as I had envisioned. It was such a success that I bought it on the spot.

When I was about to make out a cheque, Seth had an urgent request: Could I please go with him to my bank to draw out the cash, as a cheque might takes weeks to clear from L.A.? I obliged him and handed over a bundle of C-notes. At that he grasped my hand and thanked me fervently: "You have just saved my pickup truck! They were going to repossess it tomorrow, so you've been a lifesaver." Obviously anyone without "wheels" in L.A. would be helpless indeed, so I became a Good Samaritan while gaining a fine sculpture.

Afterword

Writing about my adventure in collecting contemporary art has given me a new perspective. A common definition of "contemporary art" is anything that has been produced within the last twenty-five years. If that definition is correct, then much of what I purchased will not fit in that category shortly. Will it then be called "modern art"? or "art by Old Masters"?

I find myself gravitating to the splendid artists I've revered for many years, buying their work directly, through dealers or at auction. Still there must be wonderful artists whose work is aesthetically exciting. I hope to reignite the old thrill of discovery while remaining true to those whose work I've always loved. I see myself as having been an amalgam of two disparate parts. I've been serious in studying and learning about many forms of art. Yet the contemporary work has been particularly rewarding. On the other hand, collecting has been a lighthearted adventure in which the spirit of chase and participation far transcended any minimal satisfaction of ownership.

After a lifetime of collecting, what would I hate to part with? An Eskimo carving of a walrus. A Han Dynasty figurine. A Sol LeWitt wall piece. A John McLaughlin painting. That could be the extent of it. But, oh, the friendships and the occasional helping hand. Those are what really count.

J. Robert Orton, Jr.
La Jolla, May 1995

Index

316